Who Wants to be a Scientist?

Scientific research is about discovering new things and applying them to improvements in life style for people and animals. But careers in science are now very demanding, requiring much more than a keen scientific mind and practical ability. If you are considering a career in research, have already embarked on your career, want to succeed and are uncertain which route to take, or need to advise, train or supervise scientists, this book should offer some helpful advice. It covers topics ranging from choosing a Ph.D. or post-doctoral position, successful interviews and preparing your CV, to managing your supervisor, giving successful talks, publishing high-quality papers and getting yourself known, as well as broad aspects of science which are so important today, including ethics and fraud, intellectual property and exploitation and disseminating science to the public.

NANCY ROTHWELL is MRC Research Professor of Physiology, School of Biological Sciences, University of Manchester.

Who Wants to be a Scientist?

Choosing Science as a Career

NANCY ROTHWELL

University of Manchester

Illustrations by Smudge

CAMBRIDGE
UNIVERSITY PRESS

PUBLISHED BY THE PRESS SYNDICATE OF THE UNIVERSITY OF CAMBRIDGE
The Pitt Building, Trumpington Street, Cambridge, United Kingdom

CAMBRIDGE UNIVERSITY PRESS
The Edinburgh Building, Cambridge, CB2 2RU, UK
40 West 20th Street, New York, NY 10011-4211, USA
477 Williamstown Road, Port Melbourne, VIC 3207, Australia
Ruiz de Alarcón 13, 28014 Madrid, Spain
Dock House, The Waterfront, Cape Town 8001, South Africa

http://www.cambridge.org

First published 2002

Printed in the United Kingdom at the University Press, Cambridge

Typeface Swift 9/13pt.   *System* QuarkXPress™   [SE]

A catalogue record for this book is available from the British Library

Library of Congress Cataloguing in Publication data
Rothwell, Nancy.
 Who wants to be a scientist? / Nancy Rothwell.
   p. cm.
 Includes bibliographical references and index.
 ISBN 0-521-81773-0 (hbk.) – ISBN 0-521-52092-4 (pbk.)
   1. Science–Vocational guidance. I. Title.
 Q147 .R68 2002
 502′.3–dc21   2002023868

ISBN 0 521 81773 0 hardback
ISBN 0 521 52092 4 paperback

My sincere thanks to Professor Mike Stock for his characteristically astute and forthright comments on this book shortly before his untimely death. It was Mike who made me want to be a scientist and helped me to become one, so this book is dedicated to him.

Contents

Preface   *page* ix

1   Introduction   1
2   Starting out in research   5
3   Getting down to research   11
4   Scientific ethics and conduct   29
5   Publish or perish?   39
6   Communication and getting known   57
7   Moving up   71
8   Responsibilities   89
9   Funding research   105
10 Who owns science?   121
11 Science and the public   137
12 Power, pressure and politics   147
13 Social aspects of science   155
14 So who does want to be a scientist?   161

Index   163

Preface

Science is a complicated business. It affects everyone, in every aspect of their life. It can be argued that anyone who tests variations on a new cooking recipe, studies a new way to manage their garden, compares different methods of travel or new mixtures of paint to decorate their home is employing scientific principles. Of course we are all influenced by science – more so now in the twenty-first century than ever. We all benefit (and sometimes suffer) from advances in technology, medicine, agriculture, often without realising.

Some choose to enter a career in science with real knowledge and commitment, others with naivety and uncertainty. This book is an attempt to highlight the good and the bad aspects of such choices, the things you need to know to get on in research, and factors which may help in making career decisions and in determining success. It could be read by those making the choice about entering research, or those in a scientific career at any level. It is written, without apology, as a personal view on what it takes to achieve success. Not everyone will share these views.

The book originated from numerous and repetitive discussions and presentations by and to scientists within and outside my own lab, about what they should and should not do to achieve success. I felt that it would save their time and mine to summarise these in written form. What sounded like an easy and brief task, grew from this. It seemed that there was too much to say. Such a book is not, and cannot, be used as a definitive text on what is needed to be successful as a scientist. I would challenge anyone to write such a book – though many could do so from a position much stronger than mine.

The inspiration to write such a book and much of the content comes from working with very excellent scientists who had not only a great passion for science, but also a real desire to train, transfer experience and impart knowledge to those who worked with them. In particular,

Professor Mike Stock was recognised by many in his field of obesity and energy metabolism as a remarkable individual. He was also an outstanding mentor who questioned and challenged, advised and informed on every aspect of science, from designing experiments and writing papers to 'why are you doing research', and 'why should it matter to the man on the street'. Most of these discussions were conducted in the pub. He encouraged me to read widely – from scientific philosophy to the Rubyat of Omar Kyam and Edward Lear. During this reading I learnt a great deal from books written by Sir Peter Medawar. Medawar had much to say about science and scientists and the quotations in each chapter are all from his work. One of these summarises my feelings about this book:

> *I have tried to write the kind of book I myself should have liked to have read before I began research.*   Peter Medawar

1

Introduction

One does not need to be terrifically brainy to be a good scientist.
Most people who are in fact scientists could easily have been something else instead.

Long gone are the days when learned gentlemen (and they were almost exclusively men) of science pondered the natural and physical world around them, and discussed the latest discoveries and inventions, often over dinner and a glass of fine wine. Even fifty years ago, science seemed a rather gentler activity than it is today. Then it seems, there was time to take tea and linger in discussions on fascinating topics. Compare this to the frenzied world of research today. In the twenty-first century we not only have to conduct successful, competitive research, but also fund it, publish it, talk about it (often to the public as well as to colleagues), patent it and exploit it – and all this while juggling the pressures of teaching and an ever-growing burden of administration. Anyone who really knows about research could be forgiven for feeling that it's a tough life for scientists – yet those outside still think we take eight week summer vacations!

Of course our 'rose-tinted view' of the scientific past ignores the struggles and challenges facing our scientific forefathers; and science offers the same, and perhaps even greater, challenges and excitement as it always did. Nevertheless, scientists now need a range of new skills, and they need to learn them quickly in order to be successful. Many universities provide courses for graduate students on communication and presentation skills, publishing, obtaining grants and fellowships, ethics and the many other aspects of research. But all too often such courses are squeezed out by the pressures of experimental work or writing a thesis, or are presented at a time when their relevance is not obvious. Even more sadly, many young scientists still have no such training, and the busy schedules of their advisors and mentors means they must acquire the skills of the trade 'by association' – or learn the hard way, by making mistakes. As you move up the career ladder, formal training is less obvious. The new faculty member is faced with the daunting task of applying for their first grant, supervising a group, training young scientists and teaching – each requiring a range of new skills and posing a set of new problems. In the past, such training was provided by 'the mentor' or supervisor, and was comparable to an apprenticeship. Today supervisors and mentors may be separate people. Supervisors have a formal position of directing research, whereas mentors may be an independent colleague who simply provides advice. If you are lucky enough to find a talented and experienced mentor, be grateful and attentive; you can learn more from them than from any book. Sadly now, few senior scientists have the time they would like to spend on either supervising or mentoring their younger charges.

This book cannot (and does not attempt to) cover all of the many issues scientists may have to deal with, nor does it offer solutions to the problems they will face. Hopefully, it may offer some practical advice on the major aspects of scientific life, which are now essential for a successful career.

2

Starting out in research

A novice must stick it out until he discovers whether the rewards and compensation of scientific life are for him commensurate with the disappointments and the toil.

All too often the choice of a scientific career or the decision to take a higher research degree is based on default. Perhaps you have a good Bachelor's or Master's degree, and you found the degree course reasonably enjoyable. After much deliberation, you still have no clear idea of the career you should pursue. Your friends are planning a Ph.D., you have the qualifications and your mentor may be quite persuasive (particularly if the department has to fill its quota award of studentships), so a Ph.D. seems like a reasonable option. The prospects of poor pay, a few horror stories of long hours and the possibility of many months with no results may dampen your enthusiasm, but in the absence of a suitable alternative, a higher degree seems a reasonable, or even an attractive option.

This is clearly not the best way to enter research, which is at best demanding, but rewarding, and at worst demoralising and unrewarding. Nevertheless, some who take this step with little commitment are still 'caught by the bug' and go on to be very successful scientists. Even the many who complete their Ph.D., but decide that research is not the career for them, should have benefited from the breadth and depth of training they receive and skills they acquire – even though they may not recognise it at the time.

Hopefully, many who undertake a Ph.D. do so because they believe that they *want* to do research, and perhaps go on to a career in some aspect of science. Even this is not an easy choice. Undergraduate projects, constrained by time and money, usually aim to teach practical skills and knowledge of the subject, and therefore give little real insight into what research is like. Some people have the fortune and foresight to take summer jobs in labs or spend a year working in a lab, and an increasing number of undergraduate courses now offer a year out working in a lab in industry or academia during the degree. These experiences are invaluable. They can help you decide if you really want to do research (or equally importantly if you do not), and are a huge bonus on your CV when applying for either a higher degree or a job – of any description.

Many universities now offer 'pre-Ph.D. courses', either as an obligatory foundation year of Ph.D. study which is very common in countries such as the USA, the DEA in France, the M.Sc. which combines lectures with a research project, or the more recently developed Master of Research (MRes) now offered by some UK universities. Each of these varies somewhat in the research training available, depending on the university and the nature of the course, but for those uncertain about undertaking a Ph.D., can be invaluable in helping to clinch the decision one way or the other. It will also provide an excellent grounding in research.

Those who go on to study for a Ph.D. are sometimes surprised that, having obtained satisfactory results during their B.Sc. or Master's projects (which may even have contributed to a publication), they struggle for many months with their Ph.D. project. This mainly reflects the very different nature of short-term projects undertaken during Bachelor's or Master's degrees, which, if the supervisor is skilled, will be designed to yield data and will often form part of a larger, ongoing project. The difference when you get to a Ph.D. is, or at least should be, that you will be tackling a much 'bigger' project (i.e. a significant scientific question) and one that will be yours. If your Ph.D. project addresses an important and novel project (which is after all what research is *really* about), it may take many months of developing methods and protocols, optimising conditions, frustrating times of dead-ends and failures. This is disheartening, especially if you have tasted some success in a smaller project. But when you do get a positive result, or perhaps even a major finding, it will (hopefully) all be worthwhile. If you are not elated by getting *that result* – and knowing that you are probably the first person to see it – then research is almost certainly not for you. The more time and effort you put in, the greater the reward when you see the data for the first time. Then you can start to build on the findings, present them to others in your lab, department and the wider scientific community, and hopefully see your name in print – knowing that the work is yours rather than just a contribution you have made to someone else's project. These real highs and lows of research are rarely experienced in short-term projects.

CHOOSING WHICH PH.D.

For many aspiring young scientists, success and enthusiasm are dependent not so much on the project they choose, but on where and with whom they work. Students all too often select their area of research on the basis of an undergraduate project or dissertation which they have particularly enjoyed. You may have strong preferences for certain areas of research (or dislike of others), but these are often based on the skills and enthusiasm of a tutor or teacher rather than on an intrinsic interest in, or on the importance of a specific subject area. Such choices can become ever-more limited with movement up the career structure, and lead to a growing reluctance to leave an area of expertise. It is sometimes unfortunate that a single, short research project can dictate the whole scientific career of the rather narrow-minded or ill-advised young scientist.

In reality, the subject area should not matter that much (within a broad subject area of science such as biology or chemistry or physics). The decision of what project to work on (at any stage in a scientist's career) should be based on whether the project is an important one: i.e. does it address interesting and important questions rather than somewhat trivial ones; does it aim to *understand* or *simply* describe scientific phenomena (the latter are often referred to rather disparagingly as 'stamp collecting', but of course have value); and, importantly, is it feasible? Some of the most exciting projects are *unfortunately* intractable – they are simply too complicated to be solved. This may be obvious even at the outset. If so, they should be avoided. Perhaps the most important way to select a good Ph.D. project is to find the right supervisor, university and department.

LOCATION

As with buying a home, the decision of which Ph.D. project is very dependent on location. Mobility and varied experience are very important in research training and careers. It is quite acceptable to stay in the same institution for an undergraduate and post-graduate degree (provided of course that it is respected and well-resourced), but if this is the case the next stage (see Chapter 7) should really involve geographical movement (if possible abroad). However, personal constraints on movement (such as family commitments) are recognised and taken into account in later appointments. In choosing a university or research institution and department, several factors need to be taken into account, but perhaps most importantly those of reputation and standing in the field. In the UK this is readily determined by checking the Research Assessment Exercise,

RAE score (Grade 4 is good, Grade 5 is excellent). Similar 'league tables' of research excellence exist in most countries, but it is important to consider the subject area in which you want to work. It is no good getting into a mediocre biology department in a university noted for its excellence in history and theology. All universities and research institutes worldwide now have excellent websites, providing detailed information of ongoing research, facilities and training for graduate students.

The nature of the Ph.D. has changed significantly over the past decade. Previously the 'apprenticeship' system prevailed, where one or two students worked side by side with a supervisor who devoted time and effort to training their students in all aspects of science. While this is still the aim, in reality most supervisors who are successful in research have several Ph.D. students, as well as other research staff to look after, and many other pressures on their time. Because of this, it is important to look at the training which may be available in the department. Are courses available specifically for graduate students? Will there be tutors or advisers to help if problems arise, or, if your supervisor is not available, is there a healthy population of graduate students to interact with? Have graduate students in the department in the past completed their Ph.D.s successfully (and on time) and secured good positions thereafter? If you cannot find this out by asking your current tutors or by searching for information, ask when you visit – any reasonable prospective supervisor will be impressed by your foresight. Although the system has changed significantly, choosing the right supervisor is just as important now as it always has been.

CHOOSING YOUR PH.D. SUPERVISOR

Of course you need to feel that you will be able to get on reasonably well with the person you will have to work quite closely with for a number of years. You must be able to communicate with them, to respect them and to feel that they will treat students fairly, even if you know they will be pushing you to work long hours and setting seemingly unattainable deadlines and goals. But ultimately they must be good scientists, ideally with an impressive record of publication, training graduate students and securing necessary funding. Selecting a newly appointed member of staff (perhaps as their first Ph.D. student) can be somewhat of a risk. But this may be balanced by the time and enthusiasm they are likely to expend.

Ask to speak to other students in the potential supervisor's lab to determine what the supervisor is like to work with. Are they enthusiastic and supportive, even when the results all seem to be negative? Do they try to ensure that their graduate students get the right training and experience to complete their Ph.D. on time, or will they keep them working in the lab long after the end of their course? Ask about the completion rates and the subsequent careers of past students, and check their publication record by a literature search. Determine if there is a good structure in the lab. For example, are there experienced post-docs who can advise on a day to day basis, and skilled technicians to help the naïve graduate student? Is the lab well funded, does it look organised and have the right equipment?

Personality and attitude to research and graduate training is important in selecting a supervisor, but if you really want to succeed in research, the supervisor's scientific achievements and reputation are of prime concern. If he or she is successful it is likely that their graduate students will also do well. Many of the world's leading scientists started out in some of the very best labs, and a significant number of Nobel Prize winners were at some stage supervised or mentored by a Nobel Laureate. The very best scientists will almost always provide the best trainers – even if they are not always the easiest people to get on with.

Reaching the right choice of a Ph.D. project or supervisor (which of course depends on each individual) may seem a daunting task. There is now a great deal of information and advice around, but if you are uncertain, there are courses which help that choice to be made, e.g. the extended Ph.D. in which the first year involves rotation between labs on several projects as is common in the US, the four year Ph.D. in the UK and some other countries or the MRes which operates a similar system. Each of these provides experience of different labs, projects and supervisors before the final choice is made for a Ph.D.

3

Getting down to research

It is psychologically important to get results, even if they are not original.

The early phase of research can be somewhat bewildering and varies considerably between countries, institutions and labs. In some institutions, the first year or so is spent on taught courses, with only short lab projects, to be followed by a gradual introduction to the research project. At the other extreme, the student is launched into their own research project on day 1 and expected to produce some results by day 3. Both approaches are valid, have benefits and disadvantages, and each poses challenges and frustrations. For any new research project there always seems to be too much to take in at once: new colleagues, new techniques, numerous papers to read – most of which seem unintelligible or at best irrelevant – talks to attend and, most importantly, results to obtain. There is so much to do and learn, but as soon as you are in the lab, try to do an experiment.

LIFE IN THE LAB

The lab is not just a physical structure, but also a group of people each acting and interacting in different and specific ways. No two lab structures are identical because they are determined by the personalities and activities of the staff, the size of the lab (people, funding and space), the type of work being undertaken and the style of the lab head. You need to know about the physical structure, the individuals, what they do, i.e. 'how the lab works'.

In most cases, active labs will include senior scientists (usually holding a faculty position in universities or senior scientists in research institutes or industry). One of these will be the lab head, but there may be several senior staff each with direct responsibility for an area of research and a group of staff/students. Post-docs are salaried staff who have a Ph.D., are usually starting to (or hoping to) attain independence. Some may already have their own funding (e.g. through fellowships) and work largely independently, while others may have only just completed their Ph.D. Graduate students (Ph.D. and Master's) can include the fresh-faced and naïve, the experienced and mature and those who are frantically writing up or trying to find a job. A large lab may have a technical superintendent or lab manager, most will have research technicians and some may have a secretary or administrative assistant. Young (and occasionally older) scientists sometimes look down on the technical, secretarial or administrative staff. This is a big mistake. They have a crucial position as 'lynch-pins' of the lab. Post-docs and grad students come and go, the skilled support staff are likely to be there much longer, are wise and experienced and normally have the trust of the lab head. It is important to establish what the roles and activities are of everyone in the lab, so, at first, watch and listen. Undergraduate students may join the lab for short projects, as part-time or summer students, and sometimes school children also gain work experience.

There are likely to be certain clear rules and other 'unwritten' ones or guidelines. With legislative issues such as health and safety there is absolutely no room for deviation or sloppiness; they will be clearly spelt out and must be strictly adhered to. Other 'codes of practice' may be less obvious. Working hours and holidays can be sticky points. In universities and research institutes, working hours are generally quite flexible for research staff, provided that you work hard and get things done. Some lab heads do have expectations on times of arrival and departure, frequency and length of lunch and office breaks and strong views on working weekends. A more realistic and common view is that it is not how many hours you are at work that matters, but what you get done. Nevertheless, there will be times you have to be there – lab meetings, seminars, etc. – and when necessary you will have to stay late, start early or work at weekends; research is not a nine-to-five activity.

THINKING AND DOING

Science is about two activities – thinking and doing. Thinking involves reading the literature, assessing current information and knowledge and major questions or problems, establishing hypotheses, designing experiments, assessing data and what they mean, writing them up and then moving on to the next set of experiments. 'Doing' is the essential part in the middle – setting up, modifying and validating techniques, conducting experiments, collecting and analysing data, preparing talks and so on. A big mistake is to try to separate thinking from doing. All too often effort on thinking is expended before and after the experiment – yet the real thinking is required *while the experiment is being conducted*. Research is normally an experimental subject (with obvious exceptions in some of the physical sciences) and depends not just on how well you plan experiments or describe the results, but on how you conduct the experimental process.

EXPERIMENTAL DESIGN

There is an extensive literature on the philosophy and historical origins of scientific practices and thinking, and in particular on how science is (or even should be) practiced and on the scientific method. The writings of eminent philosophers such as Bacon, Kant and Popper provide an important, if somewhat challenging base for any young scientist. But many twenty-first century scientists take a more pragmatic approach to what are, after all, the most important aspects of research: observation, experimental design, deduction and interpretation.

One of the fundamental aspects of scientific philosophy is that it is virtually impossible to *prove* anything is true – you can only establish beyond reasonable doubt. This is a significant problem for scientists in talking about their discoveries to non-scientific audiences, but it is also worth remembering in your experiments and writing. Experiments do not prove that your hypothesis is correct, they can only support it. The basis of modern science is the 'null hypothesis' – we try to show that something is not false. This can sound like semantics, but it is important for scientific thinking, explanation, analysis and presentation. The null hypothesis (as we so often forget) is also the basis of statistical analysis. We tend to think that statistics prove that experiments show what we predicted (or hoped for), but in reality they simply tell us about the probability that we are wrong – an important distinction. It is always worth trying to prove that your idea or hypothesis is wrong (however much you want it to be right). You can be sure that if you do not, your critics – Ph.D. examiners, referees of your paper or grant application – will do their hardest to prove you wrong, so better to be there first.

Much of science is based on hypotheses. We consider current knowledge and observations, establish a hypothesis to explain these, then determine if further observations fit the hypothesis. But of course it is not always like this. Science also depends on simply observing and describing

– without any hypothesis. Hopefully the thinking behind these observations is based on some logic and thought. Thus, archaeologists know where to look and roughly what they hope to find, but cannot necessarily predict what they will dig up; similarly epidemiological studies or multiple gene expression analyses are not hypothesis-based, and often yield surprising findings. Observation and analysis are an important first step. Yet research that explains how or why rather than what (i.e. it tells us the mechanisms) is generally more highly regarded than descriptive studies.

We tend to think of science as a logical and planned activity, yet much of what is discovered is surprising and unpredictable. This unexpected nature of science (which is what makes it so exciting) is discussed eloquently by Wolpert (see end of this chapter). Imagination and lateral thinking have value in science as well as in arts. This is not to undermine the importance of scientific rigour, observations and careful analysis, but always look for and think about the unexpected.

As a starting point you need to decide what the problem or question is that you are trying to address or answer. This may seem so obvious that it is hardly worth mentioning, but so often we lose sight of the primary objective within the enormous detail of experiments. Thus, where possible, the simplest experiments are often the most revealing. Many scientists begin to design better experiments when they start to write formal grant applications to obtain funds for research. In grant proposals it is necessary to clearly describe (and therefore think about) the hypotheses, objectives and questions, then discuss how they will be tested or achieved experimentally (see Chapter 9) in a logical order. It is worth thinking about every experiment in the same way.

Most research projects will involve 'big questions' and 'little questions', i.e. the overall, long-term objectives, which are then broken down into a series of experiments which test specific aspects of the hypothesis or perhaps provide the necessary ground work. Having established the questions, it is necessary to decide if they are *testable* experimentally. Some problems are simply too big to address realistically within any a project (or even a lifetime), such as 'how does the brain work?'. But they can be approached in small steps. Even more simple scientific questions might not be answered by a specific series of experiments. The reasons for this include poor experimental design, the number of confounding variables or the absence of the necessary tools. Such problems are particularly common with complex systems, such as whole organisms, ecological systems or major geological questions. Here, some assumptions will have to be made in designing the experiments, and the assumptions will not always be correct. The number of uncontrolled or potentially confounding variables will present a major challenge in trying to design the 'clean' experiment to test a specific hypothesis. Often a long series of experiments will be required to address the complexities. Sometimes there is a fine balance between deciding that experiments really cannot answer your questions and the problem is simply intractable or the system too complex. This must be balanced against the pragmatic approach. It may be necessary to conduct experiments which you are aware cannot fully answer a question, but will provide a potentially valuable contribution. An awareness of the limitations (and taking account of these in any conclusions made from the data) may be better than simply 'talking yourself out of the experiment'. You have to start somewhere. A common example of this is with genetically modified animals. Deletion of a specific gene (often in the mouse, *Drosophila* and other organisms) has proven a valuable approach for detecting the function and importance of the gene product. Yet the results may be influenced by compensatory changes during development, effects of the genetic modification independently of the specific gene deletion, unexpected actions of the gene product and influences such as genetic background, gender and environment. All of these can and have led to false conclusions. But, while such influences must be considered, in the end many such experiments have proven extremely valuable.

The design of each experiment will be different, but the principles will be similar: e.g. does it include the relevant control, reference or, in the case of clinical studies, placebo groups (in some cases there will need to be several); are the number of independent observations sufficient for valid statistical analysis; are the conditions optimal; can you rely on the reagents, equipment and methods? The simplest experiment involves the relevant control and a single test group. It will normally be necessary to conduct preliminary experiments to ensure that the concentrations, time course, the tools used, etc. are appropriate. Do not just believe the information provided by the manufacturers about the reliability or robustness of a tool, technique or piece of equipment – they are likely to be over optimistic.

In the desire to optimise experiments, failure to assess critically each step in the procedure could lead to unnecessary efforts being spent on trivial aspects. There is little point in measuring one parameter to a high accuracy when the final result will be influenced by an interacting parameter that is inherently variable or cannot be assessed accurately (accuracy and reliability are not the same). So, for example, in an experiment to measure the food intake of animals, there is little point in weighing the food presented with great precision if you do not account for the potentially large and variable amounts of food spilt at the bottom of the cage. Think about the key, limiting steps in any measurement, then focus on optimising those.

NEW METHODS, EQUIPMENT, TECHNIQUES, TECHNOLOGIES

Even the most experienced researcher will (or should) be continually thinking about new technologies, equipment and approaches to tackle their scientific questions. The pace of technological development is frighteningly fast, but for those early in their research career it should be easier to adapt to new techniques and to be innovative than it is for the old die-hards. At first, new techniques are learnt from others (usually in the same lab) who have experience and proven success, but occasionally a new Ph.D. student will start by developing a technique previously untested in their lab.

Learning a technique means following accurately a prescribed protocol or published method, checking it at each stage, handling all aspects of the experimental process with attention and care and always being on the look out for something going wrong. But, technical skills and the ability to follow a given protocol are not enough. It is essential to know the basis of the technique – the principles underlying the measurements, what they can and do show – and most importantly the limitations. It is not usually essential to understand the fine detail of how each piece of equipment works or every aspect of the development process. When a sophisticated and expensive piece of equipment breaks down it is rare that the young scientist will be expected (or even allowed) to set forth with the manual and a screwdriver. That is usually a job for the expert – if possible from the company that makes the equipment, so that the warranty is not infringed. However, when asked in a viva, after a scientific presentation, or even in a general (and seemingly informal) discussion, why a specific technique was chosen, about the reasoning behind any modifications or the thinking behind the analysis, an answer such as 'that is what I was told to do', or 'that is what others who have published did', is not acceptable. You must know why, and be able to justify what you have done. For many measurements, a range of different techniques are available, each of which has obvious (or sometimes subtle) advantages and disadvantages. It is important to know what these are and to be aware of the limitations of any approaches you use.

GREEN FINGERS

Everyone comes across the scientist with 'green fingers'. They may be a technician, a Ph.D. student or an experienced researcher who always seems to get techniques working well, manages to solve the problems where others have failed and can obtain data. This success is due in part to care and attention, manual dexterity, practice and experience. Failure to pay attention to detail, sloppy techniques or clumsiness are sure ways to hinder even the best research project. Some techniques require more care than others, some just take practice, but all require thought. Often it is necessary to discard your first set of data (however valued they may be) because you are still on a 'learning curve'. Most people will come across, or work with, scientists who are not simply careful and precise, but also seem to be 'lucky'. Their experiments work when yours fail, they come up with the exciting and often unexpected result and they can be the subject of considerable envy. Of course there is some luck in research – the chance of being in the right place at the right time, and a large proportion of major breakthroughs result from the unexpected. But in fact luck is only a small part of success in research; the real key is seeing the unexpected and recognising what it means. The frequently quoted story of Alexander Fleming's 'chance' discovery of penicillin, when spores wafting through an open lab window supposedly landed on his plates and killed the bacteria he was growing, has almost certainly been greatly exaggerated and embellished. The key fact was that Fleming *noticed* something unusual which others may have ignored or missed. The saying that 'chance favours the prepared mind' is highly applicable to research.

'Green-fingered' scientists do well because they *think* about what they are doing – always trying to see a problem as soon as, or, if possible, before it arises. This is particularly difficult when conducting routine or mundane measurements. They are quick to spot something that does not look quite right, note down anything that is unusual, compare each experiment with the earlier ones to ensure consistency and, if in doubt, to stop and re-evaluate. This is what you need to do. Always be on the look out for the unusual and unexpected; it is this rather than the predicted or the normal result which may hold the key to a breakthrough. Of course just looking and checking is not enough – judgement is required. You need to judge which are the crucial steps in a protocol (i.e. the ones that require special care and accuracy), rather than spending many hours on procedures for which precision is not so important. Sometimes unexpected factors make all the difference between success or failure – the order in which experimental steps were undertaken, which room the measurements were performed in or even (as I found from painful personal experience) the time of year. Think about the inherent errors in each stage of a protocol – there is usually little point in measuring one step to an accuracy of 0.001% when the unavoidable variation in another is greater than 1%. Distinguishing between the expected result, one which is due to error or normal variation and one which reveals exciting, new information is more difficult – particularly for the inexperienced. In the latter cases at least it is important to record everything and discuss it with someone more experienced. Usually it will be discarded or left unexplained, but sometimes it can be valuable, even many months later. Above all else look out for the unexpected.

ORGANISATION AND MANAGING YOUR TIME

Research may start off slowly, but it will not stay that way for long. Fairly soon it will be necessary to balance experiments (which as a general rule take twice as long as you expect), learn new methods, analyse data, write reports and papers, prepare talks, attend meetings and seminars, advise and supervise others and, in a few precious and snatched moments do what is most important – to *think* about what you are doing, where you are going and what you have found.

Some manage this growing work load and conflicting demands simply by working longer hours, cutting coffee and lunch breaks and slogging through each weekend. Such heroic dedication to science will be necessary at times, but the first and best approach to the problem of managing time (or lack of it) is planning and organisation. Get a diary – whether paper or electronic does not really matter, but write in it everything you have to do and attend (this is also important to ensure that you do not miss important meetings). Review your diary regularly – not just for that day, but for the weeks ahead – so you can see when a deadline is coming up for submission of an abstract or when you have to prepare a talk or a report. Your diary (or other books) should also be used to take notes, store contact numbers, names, etc., though all experimental information should go into your lab book. Many people find it helpful to have a 'meetings' note book for recording information from seminars, discussions with your supervisor, etc., and this may also be used to put down ideas and thoughts. Again, review this regularly. The significance of some of the information gleaned from a seminar, sudden ideas or experimental observations may not be recognised until much later.

When planning experiments, allow plenty of extra time – things often go wrong, and many will have to be repeated. It is useful to have deadlines for completing a series of experiments and writing a paper, but these need to be realistic – only rarely do things go quicker than you imagine, and there will be interruptions. *Think* in advance about everything that will be needed for your experiment, so that it is not delayed at the last minute because one of the reagents has run out or you forgot to book the equipment. Go through each stage, checking what will be needed and ensuring that there will be minimal interruption. This is generally much easier for graduate students and young scientists who do not have the added demands of administrative duties, teaching, talking to students with sudden problems, managing research staff, or writing papers or grant applications or administrative duties. Learn to deal with interruptions at the outset and things will be much easier later. If someone needs to speak to you, explain what you are doing and ask if you can arrange a time later, organise meetings at times when you are available to talk.

Allow some time to deal with paperwork – to read papers, check emails, deal with correspondence or return phone calls. Do not let these pile up on your desk – act on them, file them or bin them. It is so easy to put something off until later, but it will take just as long to deal with then as now, and by that 'later' time you may be even busier. Learn to file and organise. This is difficult for naturally untidy people, but becomes more essential as life gets busier. Design an effective filing system for paper documents, electronic files, emails, addresses, contacts, etc. – this will all save time later. Making lists of urgent and important things can also be helpful as an *aide memoire*, and in prioritising. It is also quite self satisfying as major items are completed and crossed off the list. Beware though, some people spend more time making lists and files than actually getting on with the required actions.

As with most things, learn from others – see how busy people deal effectively with demands on their time. You will see a few who miraculously manage from under a huge pile of paper and seem to know exactly where everything is. This is a rare talent and not an example that is generally useful to follow. It is much better to see how incredibly busy people manage to keep their desk tidy, handle numerous and often conflicting demands, yet always seem to find time for the main research tasks.

There will be times when things get too much – you simply cannot do everything. Sit down for a few minutes and *prioritise*. Sometimes it is easier to do the trivial or simple jobs first, when in reality they could be dropped so that just one major, but important task can be completed. Be realistic when deciding whether to take things on. It may be flattering to be asked to give a talk or supervise a student, but think whether you really can do it before accepting. Rather few people are naturally organised and efficient, but most learn by experience and observation. Try to learn *before* real chaos sets in!

WORKING WITH OTHERS

Research may involve many hours of working alone, but it is also highly dependent on working with others. This can be one of the real pleasures of science. The lab, the department and the bigger scientific scene all depend on interaction between people. Find out, as early as possible, the 'dos and don'ts' – which equipment you do not touch without specific authority, how you dispose of waste, who is in charge of safety, whether playing the radio is approved or frowned upon, and many other of the interactions of lab life? Most of the equipment and space in the lab will be communal (though you may be allocated your own bench space and some equipment). It is important to respect all equipment and facilities – do not just walk away when the printer jams, the distilled water runs out or the pH meter breaks down. Everyone in a lab has collective responsibility. Do not assume that tedious tasks such as cleaning up the lab are the technicians' jobs – join in with even the most routine and trivial tasks and you will gain considerable respect.

In successful labs, people help each other, and as a newcomer you will rely on the goodwill and support of others. Ensure that you offer similar help and support wherever possible. You may be asked to help with supervision of someone more junior, perhaps an undergraduate or a visitor. Give your time generously, but if the help required becomes unreasonable, discuss it with your supervisor.

In most groups of people working closely together, problems can arise. Maybe one individual seems particularly difficult to get on with, or there is a personality clash; you may feel that someone is favoured by your supervisor; or that the unreasonable behaviour of others is having adverse effects but is going unnoticed by the lab head. Try to stay outside such personal difficulties as much as possible and avoid gossip or taking sides. But, if the problem is significant, try to (without overt complaint) talk tactfully to a senior member of the lab or the lab head.

Getting on with others in a lab is more challenging for someone who is not in their own country and perhaps has a different language. Cultural differences can have a significant impact on the way people behave towards each other and language differences may be a significant barrier. Patience, understanding and respect for those of a different background or culture will help enormously, and a warm welcome to newcomers of any origin is usually repaid later.

Socialising is an important aspect of any group. This does not necessarily mean you have to spend all your free time with the other members of the lab, but some participation usually helps. As you gain experience, think of the new members of the lab (particularly those who are not in their own country) and invite them for lunch, a drink or just a chat.

MANAGING YOUR SUPERVISOR

If you have chosen your lab and supervisor well, they will support and help you, but it is important to remember that, if they are successful, they will be very busy – the more successful and eminent they are, the busier they will be. The onus is always on the lab head to manage and supervise projects, staff and students, but if you help them they will help you. It is important to optimise your interactions with them, to know how to make their lives easier and how to interact with them so that you both benefit.

First, observe and learn. Does the lab head welcome interruptions and regular updates on results, problems and concerns, or do they prefer pre-arranged meetings and written reports? Do they work by email? What are the best (and worst) times to approach them? For some, mornings are better, for others later in the day. The supervisor–student relationship is extremely important. Each needs to get to know the other, and appreciate and understand how they work and feel. This information may be gleaned from others in the lab, by watching what happens or by asking. Do not be afraid to ask your supervisor directly whether they would like to see each result as it is obtained or a summary at pre-arranged meetings, and how they like to focus meetings. Do they really want to be disturbed by emails and faxes when they are abroad, or phone calls at home for something less than a dire emergency?

For the busy group leader, written summaries of experimental plans, results and their interpretations, and summaries of recent publications, or the plans for your own papers can be very useful. Stick to deadlines. If you agree on a date to produce a draft of a paper or a summary of data, keep to it. Your supervisor should do the same, but may have many other pressures and will usually be busier than you are. If you cannot meet a deadline you cannot expect a response from them. If they are very busy, try to arrange a time to discuss things – look at how long you will need and make sure you remember the appointment. It is very annoying to someone who has almost every minute of their diary filled and schedules carefully planned, to find that a graduate student simply 'forgot' the planned meeting. If you find you need to discuss something unexpectedly (whether good or bad), tell your supervisor that you appreciate they are busy, but if they have a few moments you would like to discuss something important. Do not interrupt ongoing meetings unless it is really urgent.

Most senior scientists will have secretaries or personal assistants who can be an enormous help to you, and must be respected and befriended! They may be able to slot times into diaries, tell you when it is a good or a bad time to interrupt, relay the mood of 'the boss' and help you to get time and attention.

When you need to discuss results, papers, thesis, oral presentations with your supervisor, make it easy for them and for you. Prepare the information well in advance – it is not reasonable to present an abstract to your busy supervisor only hours before the deadline for submission and expect they will always have, or can make, the time to consider it carefully. It is sloppy, inconsiderate and unprofessional to expect senior scientists to correct your English, presentation style or format. It also suggests you lack pride in your work and professionalism.

Occasions may arise when you have something serious and important to discuss – perhaps your future career, real depression and despair with your work, serious personal grievance or major concerns about your research or that of others. Let your supervisor know in advance that you have something important to discuss and ask for a reasonable length of time to discuss it. Whenever possible try to present *solutions* rather than *problems* – even if the solutions are not perfect it will show that you recognise the difficulties and are trying to address them. People who do nothing but complain (even if they have some grounds) are often avoided and labelled as 'trouble-makers'. Sometimes, even after such discussions, you may feel that your supervisor has been disinterested, unfair or uncaring. Think carefully about whether his or her response is justified and, if you feel it is not, ask to see another senior member of staff in confidence, but be aware that you may be putting that member of staff and your supervisor in a difficult position. It may be necessary, and fully justified, but does require some forethought. In many cases the second person will respond in a similar way.

DATA RECORDING

Everything you do and every piece of data you obtain must be recorded – even though at the time it may seem trivial. It is remarkably easy to find you have forgotten a few essential details several months later, and surprising how what seemed at the time to be copious and legible notes are later found to be incomplete or illegible. Approach data recording in a way such that anyone else could repeat what you have done from your records without speaking to you and as though your notes are public property which, as we will see later, they usually are (Chapter 9).

Lab books are still the most common form of written record, in spite of the presence of a computer in every lab. Write down your plans and protocol (unless it is described adequately elsewhere), record every piece of data and even include your thoughts about an experiment or data, noting in the protocol or the results anything unusual. Keep original records or printouts and fix them into the lab book. For certain aspects of research and development (e.g. in industry where potential new medicines are being studied) absolutely everything must be kept – even the scraps of paper on which the settings of the machine or the weights of compounds are scribbled (see Chapter 9). Note the manufacturer, catalogue number, date of arrival of each material used in your experiment. Keep a record of whether a slightly different piece of equipment was used or some part of the experiment was performed by someone else. Each of these, seemingly trivial pieces of information, may be important if you need to explain an unexpected result, or if the batch or source of material changes.

Large amounts of data are stored electronically in numerical format, as graphics and figures or as photographic images. Keep a careful index of all files, ideally in your lab book; mark each file in a logical sequence, with a footer which will identify its location, the experiment number and the nature of the information; and *always* keep a back up – the general rule is that the more important the information, the more likely it is that the disc will be lost or the hard drive will become corrupted. More than one Ph.D. student I have supervised has lost a major part of their thesis through a virus, a corrupted disc or an inadvertent delete command.

DATA PRESENTATION AND ANALYSIS

Presentation and analysis of results will present challenges. The results of most experiments will be analysed objectively and presented in a summarised format, such as the mean or median, together with the number of observations in the group and an indication of the variation (e.g. range, standard error or standard deviation). Simple arithmetic means (even with associated variation) may not reveal the true nature of your data. They will not show if the distribution is similar between groups, or if there are one or two 'outliers' that 'skew' the data. Unless you are a real expert it is worthwhile consulting someone who is expert in statistical analysis. The usual advice is to see the statistician during the stage of designing experiments, *before* beginning them. This is certainly worthwhile and may help to determine the size of each group (i.e. the number of observations) required in order to detect statistically significant differences of a given magnitude. This *power analysis* is now required by many funding bodies, particularly where animals are being used, since it provides an indication of the minimum number of observations necessary to establish differences of a defined magnitude. However, power analysis requires some knowledge of the expected data – the distribution and variation and the predicted difference between two treatment groups, which very often can be obtained only *after* experiments (at least preliminary ones) have been undertaken.

Statistical analysis is the bane of many scientists' lives, particularly in biological and biomedical research. It is often applied at a time when the relevance is not obvious, and misused widely in practice. Expert statistical advice not only puts you on the right track, but also provides good answers to later criticism from examiners, editors and referees. It is rarely necessary to become knowledgeable about the intricacies of statistical analysis or to remember the formulae for each test, but it is essential to know what each statistical test can and cannot do, when they should be used and when they are inappropriate. Very different tests must be applied to data sets depending on whether the distribution is normal, the variance of each group is equal, on the sample size and the number of treatments. If in doubt, seek advice – and keep asking, the next set of experiments may be very different.

It is very tempting to omit data points which do not seem to fit with the rest of the group or to try a different statistical test if the first does not give the expected or hoped-for result. Such '*data manipulation*' is not acceptable and can even borderline on fraud (see Chapter 10). Data can of course be omitted, but only when the criteria for omission are established *before* the results are obtained (e.g. if values lie outside a specified range), and the same data omissions must be applied rigorously to every group. Statistical analysis is required of most data, but it can result in you losing sight of the real significance of their findings. A statistically significant difference may in fact be so small as to have little *scientific* significance. In some cases (e.g. large clinical trials) a difference between groups of a few percent is important, but in many experimental systems it could be of little relevance. Statistics are important, but as I was advised by a very wise, elderly scientist, you only have to weigh one mouse and one elephant to believe that they are different! Similarly, while 5% is usually taken as the acceptable level of chance (i.e. probability of < 0.05), there is nothing magical about this figure, and of course it means that from twenty random measurements you are always likely to see some difference. Even with the most appropriate statistical analysis, many results can lead to erroneous conclusions because of chance as well as poor experimental design.

One way around the complexities of statistical analysis is to present the raw data, either as individual data points, or as photographic images – indeed the latter is used extensively to show electron micrographs, immunohistochemistry, in situ hybridisation, etc. The problem here is whether the reader can be certain that the pictures presented are truly representative of all the data obtained, even though they are always described as such by the author. No one puts in their worst picture, and space and cost limitations often prohibit numerous photographs. Nevertheless, it is important to keep all pictures, just in case the data are questioned or the examiner or referee makes a (quite reasonable) request to see other examples. With digital scanning and image enhancement programmes, keeping original data is more important then ever.

Subjectivity so often creeps into research and must be minimised. Wherever possible interventions should be made 'blind', so that the investigator is not aware of the experimental groups, and someone independent keeps a code of the treatments or experimental manipulations until after all the data have been obtained. This is an essential requirement for clinical trials of new drugs, surgical or medical interventions, but is not applied as rigorously in experimental lab work. It is particularly important if the nature of the measurements may lead to subjectivity, a grading of the severity or strength of a signal based on the *judgement* of the observer rather than objective analysis. In addition to 'blinding', some of the judgements on selected observations should be checked by an independent observer who does not know the details of the experiment or the predicted results.

SCIENTIFIC CRITIQUE, DISCUSSION AND DEDUCTION

When, at last, you are the proud owner of your first results, they will be looked at, thought about, discussed (with your supervisor, fellow students and perhaps at lab meetings) and inevitably criticised. This procedure is an essential part of research, but can also be a major blow. Some young scientists have an entirely realistic, or even pessimistic view of what is required to complete a study or write a paper, but many set off thinking that in just a couple of months their first paper will be complete. This is rarely true. However, supervisors should not try to dampen the optimism and enthusiasm of the young – it is a great asset and quite refreshing. Indeed, many senior scientists claim that an important reason why they remain in academic institutions (even with the rather poor pay) is because of their interactions with excited and enthusiastic young scientists, who will of course eventually learn – the hard way – that only rarely do results come quickly and easily. Some young scientists have the opposite approach – they are never satisfied with what they have found. This latter approach is commendable, but can also be impractical, and even negative, if taken to extreme. Whatever the prospective view of what the experiments will show and the data reveal, critical evaluation of what is *actually obtained* is essential.

There is always a danger in over-interpreting results. If possible, put yourself in the position of your most rigorous critic – *look for what is flawed or misleading or incomplete*. At first such critique will be the job of the supervisor – and some are notoriously over-zealous about limited or incomplete data and will always want more. Discussion of research findings with the rest of your research group is helpful, but the ultimate test is the wider scientific community and how they view your findings when you speak publicly about the work or try to publish (Chapters 5 and 6). It is far better that the errors and omissions are seen by colleagues and friends than exposed to the sometimes critical, and even occasionally hostile, world outside.

Discussion of what results show (and equally importantly *fail to show*) is one of the most critical stages of research, and one which requires experience, time and effort. Many hours of experiments and fruitless endeavours can be spared by critical discussion. Having completed experiments, you need to decide what to do next. Deduction is the process of determining what you have, what it means and where to go with the next experiments. This process is an essential part of science and training in research and needs to be demonstrated in your thesis or paper. Designing and conducting an experiment can be compared to experimenting with a good recipe. The key to real culinary (and scientific) success is to recognise when something is wrong, establish how to rectify it, or to tease out the elements of success and move forward. Science is usually more complex than cookery (and rather less subjective). In science you are attempting to understand the unknown, and in most cases compete with those who have the same goal.

DISAPPOINTMENT AND STOPPING

Anyone involved in research for some time will have experienced failure – whether this is due to personal error, equipment or materials which are not optimal – the beloved hypothesis proved wrong. Research will (and should) include disappointment. Enthusiasm and optimism, backed with a dose of realism is essential, but this has to be tempered. It seems difficult to plod on with a project which keeps yielding negative data or is fraught with technical problems. To continue enthusiastically is highly commendable, but in reality your hardest decision is when to stop the project and call it a day. This is normally a difficult, perhaps traumatic choice and one which requires discussion. You may be unwilling to give up on what seems to have been an enormous effort and major part of your life, or your supervisor may be pushing you to continue with what you think is a fruitless or misdirected approach. It may help to discuss the project with others within or outside the lab. Ultimately it is necessary to decide when to cut your losses and move on.

Some of the issues discussed above may make the lab sound like a daunting place with problems waiting around each corner and the supervisor an ogre. This is far from the truth. The vast majority of researchers are friendly people who are fun to work with and research in the lab is a most enjoyable experience. Nevertheless, it is always worth being aware of what *could* go wrong, even though hopefully it never will.

FURTHER READING

On Being a Scientist (1996). Washington, DC: National Academy Press.
Wolpert, L. (1992). *The Unnatural Nature of Science*. London: Faber & Faber.
Medawar, P. (1961). *The Strange Case of the Spotted Mice*. Oxford: Oxford University Press.

4

Scientific ethics and conduct

A scientist who habitually deceives himself is well on the way toward deceiving others.

Philosophically, scientific research is about discovering the truth, so dishonesty should have no place. However, scientists are normal people with the same faults and failings as anyone else, with inhibitions and fears, and, in spite of the lofty morals of science, some do behave badly, committing acts of dishonesty. Many more would consider themselves basically honest, but good intentions do not always ensure ethical behaviour.

The responsibilities of scientists are far reaching. You have responsibilities to colleagues and the scientific community, your employer and funder, and of course to society. Unfortunately, the limits of ethical behaviour and good conduct are not always obvious. Only rarely is the young scientist handed a set of rules and regulations as they begin to train in research. They will (or should) be aware of general moral and legal issues, and things they should not do, such as steal goods, harm people or lie about what they have done. But scientific conduct is rather more complex than that. Whereas it may be acceptable in some professions to be 'economical with the truth' (i.e. to simply leave something out or unsaid if it benefits your cause), this is not so in science.

The number of cases of overt misconduct (which is proven) seems to be relatively small, but growing. The apparent growth may be simply that there is now more awareness, investigation and publicity about such cases. There is no doubt that people like to hear about a good scandal, and the reports of scientific misconduct in journals, such as *Science* and *Nature*, are likely to attract a greater readership than some of the scientific papers. However, there is real concern that many cases of misconduct are undiscovered, and that the size of the problem is underestimated. Indeed in many cases no actions (apart from distaste by colleagues) would be taken.

BEING FAIR

An important aspect of scientific behaviour is fairness to those you work with, and a major source of contention between even the best intended, is acknowledgement of credit. Research these days tends to be conducted by teams of people, each making varied contributions and each hoping for acknowledgement and recognition. These issues apply not only to authorship (and the order of authorship) of published work (see Chapter 5), but also to acknowledgement of contributions in oral presentations and informal discussions.

The issues of due credit are complex and best dealt with by open discussion, but cases of someone claiming that they have done the work themselves when in fact another has contributed significantly is clearly unacceptable. It is natural to try to promote your own work or that of your own group and the practice of 'self citation' (i.e. quoting mainly your own published work while ignoring that of others) is common, but rarely goes unnoticed, and often has unfortunate pay backs. If you fail to acknowledge the major contributions of others you cannot expect them to recognise you.

Being fair also means being as open as possible and sharing what you have whether this be reagents, data or thoughts (see Chapter 10). There may of course be limitations on such openness due to confidentiality issues or the fear of a competitor beating you to it. However, no matter what the disadvantages, these are far outweighed by the advantages.

CONFLICT OF INTEREST

Science is a relatively small world and, as you move up, it is likely that you will be reviewing or influencing the publications, funding, appointment and promotion of those that you know well and who may even be close friends. This can pose significant problems for professional behaviour and conflict of interest. Loyalties may be strong, but fairness and openness is essential. The more powerful the position you are in, the greater the potential for abuse of that power and for influencing decisions (sometimes even subconsciously) to your own benefit or those close to you (see Chapter 12). The options here are clear: first declare any interest, then, having done so, act as objectively as possible. In declaring your involvement or association, others can judge whether your recommendations may be influenced by subjectivity. Declarations of conflict of interest apply when relatives, close friends, members of your own department and current collaborations are involved. In such circumstances you should normally decline to review a paper or a grant application and leave the room during sensitive discussions. In other cases, the association may be less obvious and down to individual judgement about declaration of possible conflict or of stepping out of the decision process. It is impossible to completely avoid subjectivity and to deny the effects of personal preferences for individuals or their research or that your behaviour may be different towards a competitor or someone you dislike. Do not assume you can hide behind anonymity – personal bias or misuse of power or position may often come back to haunt you.

EXPERIMENTAL MISCONDUCT

Anyone with some experience in research will have obtained an experimental result. This may be just the one you were hoping for, but then, despite extensive efforts, you are unable to repeat the experiment and get the same result. Worse still is when *someone else* cannot repeat your results. This variation and discrepancy is common and due to many factors, such as small differences in experimental protocol, natural variations and, unfortunately, sometimes to scientific misconduct.

Misconduct can cover a range of practices, but it is important to distinguish those which result from *intent* and those (much more common) that are due to unintentional behaviour. The latter would include genuine human error, perhaps due to ignorance, lack of experience or fatigue, to 'sloppiness' or to unintentional bias (see below). These are not acceptable in good science, but are usually understood and sometimes inevitable. Within this category, but more serious, is the truly misguided behaviour where a scientist has such a strong commitment to his hypothesis or idea that his or her judgement becomes coloured – i.e. he wants the experiment to work so much that his or her behaviour (perhaps unknowingly) is influenced. The most common examples of this are in cases of omission – leaving out things that do not fit with expectations or hope – though this can also come under the category of overt fraud. Protestations that you did not realise or mean to do it are no defence.

BIAS

Scientific experiments should be designed to show that your hypothesis is wrong, and should be conducted completely objectively with no possible subjective influence on the outcome. Unfortunately few, if any, scientists are truly objective. They have often decided long before the experiment is begun what *they would like the* result to be. This means that very often bias is (unintentionally) introduced into the experiment, the experimental procedure or the interpretation of results. It is all too easy to justify to yourself why an experiment which does not fit with your expectations should be ignored, and why one which provides the results you 'hoped for' is the right one. This can be partly avoided by conducting experiments 'blinded' and by asking others to check your data or repeat experiments.

'Data manipulation' (whether intended or not) is probably the commonest type of misconduct. For example there is a great temptation to omit outlying results which increase variation or influence the mean, often because the investigator has convinced him or herself of a good reason to do so. Of course, data should sometimes be omitted, but only when the criteria are well established *before* the study is undertaken or the reason is so obvious and agreed by everyone involved. Statistical analysis is another area of potential abuse and misconduct, though it should not be if good advice is adhered to. There is sometimes a temptation to 'select' the statistical test which is most likely to yield the result you were expecting (even when this is not the most appropriate), or even worse to 'try out' several tests to see which one looks best. A way to avoid such activities (even when gross misconduct was not intended) is to try to maintain *objectivity*. Stay 'blinded' to what each manipulation is as much as possible, and get others (who have no direct involvement) to look at and analyse your data (see Chapter 3).

Whether false results arise from error, sloppiness or unintentional bias, these may not become apparent until after a paper has been submitted or published. In this case, it is necessary to retract all or part of the results, usually by writing to the journal and publishing an erratum. This is embarrassing and can be quite damaging, but is much better than someone else finding out the error and publishing it.

PLAGIARISM

Plagiarism is presenting the work of others as your own. As school children we learn that copying the homework or exam answers of others is cheating and likely to carry a severe reprimand. Overt cases of blatant plagiarism are not very common in science, not least because they are relatively easy to detect, and few are so stupid as to use the work of others in a form that is unaltered, though this can and does happen.

Reproduction of the ideas, results or written work of others and presenting them as your own constitutes serious misconduct, and published work which is reproduced without permission (from the publisher as well as the author) usually contravenes copyright law. The work of others can be reproduced in your own publications, but this requires formal permission and clear acknowledgement. Indeed even using your own text, figures or other information in a publication (e.g. a review) when this has been published previously requires permission from the publisher of the original article. Cases of overt plagiarism usually occur when work is lifted from somewhat obscure publications (e.g. in another language) and is unlikely to be detected.

Plagiarism is not always so obvious and may not always be intended. For example, it is a common practice to present an excellent summary diagram published by others in an oral presentation (e.g. as a slide), in teaching or on a web site. These can also be viewed as infringement of copyright, but when the source is clearly acknowledged (ideally on the slide), it is normally seen as flattery rather than theft. The dividing line may depend on how public the presentation is. For example within a small, private group there is unlikely to be concern (or even detection). More public use of such information (e.g. on a web site) risks claims of infringing copyright or even plagiarism.

The most difficult cases of plagiarism arise from use of information divulged to an individual through a confidential source, such as a submitted manuscript or grant application or even in private conversation. Information within manuscripts or grant proposals which you are asked to review is confidential and cannot be used and certainly not reproduced. Either action could result in public disclosure and a ban on publication in the journal or refusal of funding from the awarding body concerned. The use of information described in conversations is not always viewed as plagiarism and is much more difficult to prove. If data or ideas are revealed at a public presentation or even in private conversation where confidentiality is not established (or a confidentiality disclosure agreement is not in place – see Chapter 10), it is reasonable to assume that others can and will use them. Science should be an open activity and anyone is free to work on areas that you tell them about. However, to work in the same area and on the ideas described to you by someone else, particularly in private, is likely to attract enemies. This can easily be avoided by discussing what you would like to do and potential collaborations (or discussion of labour) with the person who gave you the ideas or information.

Sometimes it is quite difficult to avoid what might be seen as plagiarism. For example, when you have to write something and have an excellent article in front of you, it will influence your thinking and writing. It is best to read the article, then put it away for a while before starting your own writing. Then check that there is not too much overlap.

FRAUD

There are clear definitions of fraud in commercial law, usually related to financial fraud, which carries severe punishment. In science, the definitions should also be clear, but are often difficult to pin down and even harder to prove. There are two general acts of fraud in science – acts of *omission* (failing to reveal information or data) and, more seriously, acts of *commission*. Both represent concealment of the truth or deception, and include attempts to mislead or overstate. Acts of commission may include fabrication or false creation. In most cases this means knowingly altering or making up results, or misrepresentation of qualifications or achievements.

The reasons for such overt acts of scientific misconduct are numerous; greed, ambition, insecurity, fear and even a desire to please the boss or funding body. The incidence of such gross misconduct is hopefully low, but of course depends on detection. Nevertheless scientific misconduct attracted sufficient concern in the USA to cause the establishment in 1990 of the Office of Scientific Integrity with the remit of reviewing and resolving cases of scientific misconduct. Their investigations have usually been quite rigorous and public.

AVOIDING MISCONDUCT

Detecting a case of severe misconduct (e.g. data fabrication) is the fear of any lab head – particularly if it occurs after the results have been published. Complete avoidance of such activity is probably unrealistic, but it can be limited.

The closer a lab head is to bench work, the more likely they are to pick up potential misconduct because they will be involved in the experiments and see the data first hand. As the lab grows, the head is likely to become more detached from the experimental work, and will rely on the summaries presented by others. It is clear that young scientists follow examples and leadership. Therefore a culture of openness, of admitting mistakes without reprimand and of recognising that many experiments will fail is essential. The temptation to discuss the expected (or hoped for) result needs to be resisted as much as possible. Young scientists (particularly from some cultures and backgrounds) may bias their results and will claim they were simply trying to please their boss and meet their expectations. For any result, it is necessary, as far as possible, to scrutinise the raw data and to encourage independent replication by someone else in the lab. It is especially important that everyone realises that their experiments will be reproduced within and, if published, also outside the lab, and that they fully understand the consequences of misconduct.

General training in scientific conduct is now becoming an important component of most graduate and post-doctoral research programmes. Such courses should deal openly with what is acceptable and what is not, even when this seems obvious. Discussion of specific examples or case studies of fraud or misrepresentation can be used to bring home the fact that even leaving out the data point which did not fit (in the absence of a good *prior* reason to do so) constitutes misconduct. Fraudulent data also have certain characteristics – they are usually less variable than experimental results which show more normal distribution, with few outliers. Fabricated data tend to show digit preference because humans select certain numbers over others, resulting in data which are not identical to normal variation.

Sometimes close colleagues (e.g. fellow students or post-docs) suspect misconduct or fraud long before the lab head is aware. This may be simply because someone's experiments 'always seem to work', because of a general suspicion, a failure by others to reproduce data or because of direct evidence. They may be unwilling to disclose this, for a variety of reasons (see below), particularly when the suspect is more senior or seen to be favoured. This failure to reveal or discuss concerns is difficult to resolve, but needs to be dealt with confidentially and with sensitivity.

DEALING WITH FRAUD

Suspicion of fraud and establishing proof are very different and extremely difficult. If you suspect a colleague (whether a fellow student, post-doc or senior member of staff) the tendency is to keep quiet, for fear that you are wrong or may suffer as a result – whether your suspicions are correct or otherwise. Disclosure of such suspicions needs to be considered carefully – how, when and to whom? The most obvious person to talk to is your immediate boss, perhaps initially just to raise a mild concern. Even then it is wise to state clearly that the discussion is in confidence, at least until you have heard their opinion and advice. Unless you have firm evidence, your claims are likely to be questioned or even disbelieved and could cause significant problems. For a lab head, avoiding action is potentially dangerous, but depends on the available evidence. Suspicions are best dealt with by reviewing raw data, getting the experiment replicated by someone else and discussing the results, in the hope that this will reveal misconduct, or at the very least limit future activities. Stick to facts rather than suspicion, and at all costs avoid persecution. When the evidence is clear and irrefutable, it is best to seek the advice of an independent senior colleague, then act quickly and firmly. Deposit all the available note books or other evidence in a safe place to avoid them being altered or 'lost'. Most institutions have formal procedures for dealing with cases of potential misconduct (of any type) which normally results in an internal (but independent) committee to review the prima facie case, to be followed by an external review to assess the evidence and determine required action.

Once suspicion of misconduct is reported, the consequences can be difficult, particularly for the individual who has made the claims – often known as the 'whistle-blower'. Unfortunately, in many public cases of reported misconduct, the 'whistle-blower' comes out as badly (or even worse) than the accused. It is only fair that this should be pointed out to the individual who points at the misconduct, but it should not be used as a case for inactivity. The difficult judgement is in deciding when a case should be formally reported to institutional authorities, to funding agencies or to national bodies (such, as in the USA, the Office of Scientific Integrity). The decision of course depends on the severity and circumstances of the case.

BROADER RESPONSIBILITIES

Scientists have a moral and legal obligation to avoid discrimination, harassment or preference towards anyone they work with, but they also have responsibility for the human subjects they may study, their colleagues and to the society in which they live and work. The last few decades has seen growing concern about issues such as genetically modified organisms, the use of live animals in research, human tissues and subjects. Each has their own scientific and public sensitivities and regulatory limitations which cannot be avoided.

In most countries, these issues are governed by extensive regulations at the institutional or national (legislative) level. Failure to meet these regulatory requirements (whether intended or not) can result in anything from severe reprimand and limits on future scientific activity, to termination of your contract of employment or criminal prosecution.

The responsibility goes much further. Each scientist has a responsibility to every individual and to the human tissue or subject that they use in their experiments. They may also be required to discuss and defend their research on such issues in the public arena to a society which may have major misgivings or violent objections to some aspects of science (see Chapter 11).

FURTHER READING

Lock, S. and Wells, F. (1993). Fraud and misconduct in medical research. *British Medical Journal* Publishing Group, London.

Marshall, E. (2000). How prevalent is fraud? That's a million dollar question. *Science* **290**: 1662–1663.

Cottingham, K. (2000). Protecting whistle blowers. *Science.* Nextwave, http://intl-nextwave.sciencemag.org

On Being a Scientist (1996). Washington, DC: National Academy Press.

5

Publish or perish?

Scientists are supposed to have an intuitive ability to write papers because they have consulted so many, just as young teachers are supposed to be able to give lectures because they have so often listened to them.

Good writing upon a subject is always shorter than bad writing on the same subject.

The real pleasure of science is discovery. You may be alone in the lab late at night, no doubt wishing you were somewhere else. Perhaps the last few months have not gone so well, but this is the crucial experiment. If it works, those hours of hard work and despair evaporate away and it all becomes worthwhile. Even if your finding is just a small piece in a very big jigsaw, it means that your hard work has paid off, you have that long-awaited result – and hopefully something publishable. Publishing data, whether we like it or not, is a key step in successful research. In academia the phrase 'publish or perish' is of course exaggerated. But realistically, however good your research may be, and however important your next paper will be (and everyone believes that their next paper will be their best), success in most areas of science rests on what you have published.

WHY AND WHEN TO PUBLISH

While science is, at least to most dedicated researchers, a personal activity, its ultimate success depends on collective effort, on the achievements and interactions of a vast community of scientists with varied and comple-mentary skills. It has been argued that this collaboration and interaction is one of the fundamental differences between science and the arts. Progress in science depends on sharing ideas, technological developments and scientific discoveries, all of which depend on communication and dialogue between scientists across the world. Communication through publication is essential for advances in science, but it is equally important for individuals. In some aspects of scientific life, for example in the commercial sector, '*publications*' may take the form of internal reports within the company, but this is no less important in moving a project forwards and developing your career. For most scientists, particularly in academic life, publication of a thesis, abstract, review or most commonly a research paper, is an essential part of a scientific career. It is needed for recognition, scientific discussion, funding, promotion and, of course, for your next job. The problem is that it is not just publishing that is important, it is also what, when and how you publish.

The primary vehicle for scientific publishing, i.e. the original, peer-reviewed, research article, requires new findings. These may include a new method, new results, data which re-evaluate or even question existing data or (in all our dreams) a major scientific breakthrough. Whatever the detail it must be *new* and *original*. Reviews of existing data are also an important form of publication (see below), but rarely attract the rigorous critique or the wide acclaim of new results – though the audience and the citations for reviews can be considerable. New data may be presented in many formats and styles, and optimising the presentation and impact of your findings can be as important as obtaining the data.

A graduate thesis will normally be rather different in style, length and content to a paper in a journal, but the principles of scientific writing are similar and there are certain rules and style to be learnt. The first is that many publications could be considered misleading They are presented as a logical and linear progression of background, hypothesis and aims, methods, results and conclusions. This is often described as 'IMRAD' (introduction, methods, results and discussion). In reality, most scientific research tends to hop around various experiments and ideas; sometimes the most exciting results arise unexpectedly from a seemingly unrelated project; the 'fundamental' experiment may be done last and the 'logical progression' of thought and scientific method might be defined well after the event. It is a lucky (and somewhat rare) scientist who can present their thesis or paper in the precise order (chronologically and intellectually) that it evolved. More often than not, the logical sequence is defined after the data have been collated. The gaps are filled in during the final stages of writing, or on occasion even later, after the reviewers or examiners have made their comments. In scientific writing, presentation is critical both in the overall scientific logic and at the more detailed level of writing.

SCIENTIFIC WRITING

Few if any scientists choose their career on the basis of their talents in literacy or ability to write, and few have rigorous training in scientific writing. The importance of this aspect of research is increasingly recognised, not only for publishing but also for preparing grant applications, internal reports and documents for teaching and administration.

As in most aspects of life, practice does not make perfect, but it helps a great deal. Many graduate courses now require formal literature reviews, transfer and progress reports and a 'mini-thesis' to be submitted part way through the course. However, beyond the Ph.D. you may be on your own, and unless you seek constructive criticism you cannot expect to receive help – other than in the form of rejection, when it is rarely appreciated. Always ask for honest evaluation of your written work, ideally from three types of person: first an 'expert in your field' (perhaps your supervisor, or a close collaborator). They will be able to offer informed advice on the scientific content. Second, ask someone who is in your broad field of interest (e.g. biochemistry, environmental biology or astrophysics) to offer comments, because they should be able to assess what you have written at a different level (i.e. is it easy to read, clear, logical and interesting?) without getting too embroiled in the detail. Finally, ask someone who is educated, literate and patient, but is not a scientist, to read it. They may be the most rigorous in spotting typographical errors, poor English, format variation and disorganisation. Parents, spouses, partners and good friends who are outside your profession are often excellent 'proof readers' – if only because they may have the dedication to plough through many pages of potentially boring text but also they can see things which you or others who are 'too close' to the work will miss.

Much has been written about scientific writing and there are many excellent texts on the written presentation of science (see Further reading at the end of this chapter), which provide detailed advice which is not that appropriate here. Writing in science is different to penning a novel or scripting an elegant literary piece of writing for the general public (see Chapter 11). For scientific publications, accuracy and precision, concise, unambiguous and impersonal presentation, clarity of style and consistency of format are essential. The greatest failings of the inexperienced are to meander in a disorganised pattern, to use far too many words and to write in a way which may be aesthetically pleasing but is open to misinterpretation. None of these approaches is helpful or acceptable for a scientific paper or a thesis. Examples are numerous, but a couple which illustrate the point are: 'Jones *et al*. determined the effect of

X on Y and showed an increase in the growth rate of Y in response to X', or, similarly, 'that X is related to Y is suggested by data demonstrating increased growth rate of Y in the presence of X'. Both are better expressed as, 'X increased the growth rate of Y (Jones *et al.*)'. In science, less is best. Do not be repetitive. Data speak for themselves so do not labour the point. Your audience will be a critical scientific community who can and want to judge for themselves. It is not only unnecessary, but also can cause irritation to say things such as, 'It is extremely interesting to note that', or 'these results are very interesting…'. This may elicit the response of, 'interesting to whom?'. Similarly, it is dangerous to overplay what you have found. To say that, 'these data are very exciting' (note data are plural), may leave the reader not only unexcited, but also annoyed by your presumption. It is fair to say that someone else has exciting data, but better to present your own results as fact. Here there is a fine balance. Do not overplay, but equally do not apologise either. If the results are not as expected it is not (or should not be) your fault. If the results really are important it will be obvious. If they disagree with published work, say so but do not be judgemental or labour the point.

Precision is something that we are often uncomfortable with in writing, but it is important when describing research. Terms such as 'most, many, sometimes, rarely, occasionally' can be used as long as you can give a value to it, e.g. 'most (70%) of cells responded'. This also means that you cannot 'hide' data. It is often useful to show 'a representative example', which everyone knows will not be your worst example. But if you cannot provide other similar data on request, you risk your paper or thesis being rejected. When discussing living organisms always state the species, whether the experiment was performed *in vivo* or *in vitro*, and that any necessary approval for animal experiments was met.

Some would say that scientific writing is clipped, clinical and logical – almost an insult to any reader with literary interests. This should not be the case. Every scientist should read widely, not only to gain factual information, but also to see how some of the most talented scientists can write concise, accurate, yet very readable works. The goal is for your reader to understand everything, see the data at their best (but presented honestly and openly), recognise how the results fit with the general field and see the implications. But all of this needs to be achieved in the least time, with little effort and in limited space – scientists are busy and editors have constraints on the number of pages they can publish.

To the young scientist this can seem a daunting task. Few have any experience in scientific writing, many are not proficient at *any* sort of writing and a few (even those who turn out to be eminent scientists) are barely literate. Do not despair – you will find your colleagues very willing to help. If you do not feel confident in asking an expert to read your first efforts, a generalist in your field may help, and at least try things out on a fellow student who may be having the same problems as you. Read out loud what you have written. This will help not only to see the flow, but also the logic, grammar and punctuation. If necessary, tape what you have written and play it back to yourself. Write in small sections and get rapid feedback. There is nothing more disheartening than writing thirty pages only to have red lines slashed across them by your supervisor. Perhaps the most important factor for success is what you do *before* you start writing.

PLANNING AND PREPARATION

The worst thing facing any writer is the blank page which glares at you, defying any progress in getting pen to paper or finger to keyboard. If only you could fill it, but, when you do, sheet after sheet goes into the bin. Make it easy for yourself – start off simply with something that you can get down on paper, such as a list of what you have (and perhaps then you will see what is missing) of each experiment plan. Get all the data together, if possible in the same format, with summaries. Write figure and table legends (even if some of them will get dumped later). Make a summary of what you have found. Then, most importantly, *make a plan*.

Plans are important for structured writing, for critical discussions and for self confidence. They give you a structure and a goal. Once you have decided *what* you are going to write, the actual writing is much easier. If you are facing something you find particularly difficult, you can choose the easy part of the plan to write first – the methods section is an obvious one. Without that plan the blank piece of paper may stay empty for a long time, or you are in danger of wandering aimlessly through the written document.

The first stage of the plan may seem obvious, but is so often forgotten – be sure of *what* you are writing and *who* will read it. Is it a thesis, a short or long paper, for a scientific or general audience? What is the required length? What journal and in what format? How much detail will you need? For each different type of writing, decide what the main message (or messages) is that you want to get across. It is easy to lose sight of the primary aims/findings when you get into the detail. After you have a brief plan of the main sections, add substance – what will go into each section and approximately how long will it be? This is where you may find you are missing important pieces of information, data or references. Even when this is achieved, it may still be too soon to start the actual writing. Discuss your plan with someone experienced – your Ph.D. mentor/supervisor or a senior colleague. Put the plan away for a few days then come back to it. Does it still look as good as it did when you first wrote it? The plan will almost certainly be revised as you write, and you will realise that it does not quite fit with what you actually want to, or can, say, but it will grow as you write and should continue to provide a scaffold.

Some people begin at the 'logical beginning' of a piece of writing (i.e. the introduction) and just work through it in sequence, but many prefer to get going with the methods or results. Most written works will need an abstract or summary which is usually written at the end – often in a hurry. It can be helpful to write the summary at the beginning. It will inevitably need to be revised and improved later, but this section (like the plan) helps to crystallise thoughts. The abstract/summary is probably the most important part of the written document. It is what will be read first and will give the reader an impression that is difficult to change. It sets the scene and tells the reader what to expect. If it is poorly written or presented, unclear or irrelevant, the reader will not be impressed.

When you are writing, think of the reader. She/he wants to get the message simply and quickly. Help them through the document with clear headings, easy and regular references to figures and tables, objective rather than subjective discussion, and clear 'sign posts'. Sign posts are often headings, but can also be brief statements at the beginning and end of sections, summarising and leading on to the next part, particularly in the discussion. They let the reader know where they are going and help to keep attention. The saying, 'say what you are going to say, say it, then say what you've said', is useful advice – provided the first and last are brief and informative, but not simply repetitive.

PRESENTATION

The current availability of word processing packages, graphics software, spell checks and reference managers are enormously helpful in writing. These can, however, lead to hours of time spent on fancy graphics and colour figures – too often a distraction from the actual business of writing. Such graphics and artwork will not hide poor writing or a lack of conclusive data. However, there is no excuse for sloppiness. Sloppy presentation such as typographical errors, varied format, missing references or incomplete data (even in the first version you give to your mentor or collaborator) sends the wrong message. Poor presentation may suggest to the reader that you are also sloppy in your science.

Decide on a format at the outset (this may be dictated by the journal) and stick to it. Work in double spacing with a reasonable and clear font (usually 12 point), number all pages, tables and figures logically, keep a running contents page, always label documents with a footer

– and back up your discs!. Make sure that the figures are in the same format; do not change the shading or colours or the presentation of statistical differences between figures.

Even when you have put in your best efforts, checked and rechecked and presented your data in the best way you can imagine, be prepared for hard criticism. When this comes from your supervisor/mentor or valued colleague it should be constructive and helpful, but from referees of your paper it may be a little harder to accept (see later in this chapter).

QUOTING OTHER WORK

A sure way to annoy a referee or examiner is failure to quote their work, particularly if it is seminal or important to the field. At best it may be construed as ignorance and a reflection of poor knowledge of the field, at worst as arrogance or intentional failure to give due credit. Knowledge and understanding of the literature is an essential part of scientific writing and of research in general. Today, the vast literature makes this a daunting task. You not only have to start reading the relevant literature early, as soon as, or ideally, before you start a project, but you also have to keep up to date. Do not expect much sympathy from senior scientists though. While they know that the field is much larger, and the literature more extensive than when they undertook their graduate studies perhaps twenty or thirty years ago, it is in many ways much easier now to keep on top of than it was when they had to read pages of hard copies of current contents, walk to the library to photocopy papers (or often read them in the library and make copious notes), store the information on 'dog-eared' cards, then type each reference, and retype it if there was an error. Most journals are now available 'on-line' through institutional or personal subscriptions, and papers can be searched rapidly by key words or author. You must keep your own up-to-date database of references in an electronic format which can be reformatted easily and used in conjunction with a word processing package. The excuse that you 'had not seen' a major paper published a few weeks before will not be met with great sympathy. Searching for key words and scanning papers is fine, but you should also look through all the major journals in your field and some general journals to check outside your key area. This helps you to see the bigger picture and any major new developments.

There is a danger with all this electronic retrieval and storage, because it is all so easy, to imagine that when a paper is safely stored in your database it is also in your brain, though in reality you have only scanned the title. Of course you cannot read everything that has ever been written in your field – unless it is a very small or very new field – so it is necessary to read papers *intelligently*. This means reading the abstract or summary carefully. This should tell you what the paper is about, the approaches used and what the experiments showed. Then you will be able to judge whether this is a key paper or one which has methods you may need to use (in which cases you will have to read it, and sometimes reread it carefully); or one that you can simply scan quickly and then store. Having read the abstract, the last paragraph of the introduction should say what the aims were, and the end of the discussion should reveal the conclusions – as long as the paper has been well written. Clear tables and figures with good legends should reveal everything about the results. Reading such papers not only gives you important information about recent work, but also helps you to see how to write and present a good paper. Reading widely (non-science as well as the scientific literature) is one of the best ways to improve your own writing – but do not believe everything you read! Even papers in excellent journals may later be proven to be wrong or only partially correct for a variety of reasons.

Reviews, particularly those in top journals, written by leaders in the field, should provide a *critical overview* of the subject. They cannot be quoted and re-quoted extensively when you write – this would suggest laziness and a failure to read the primary papers. Remember also that a review is likely to be at least twelve months out of date so check for the most recent references quoted in each review. Chapters in multi-author books are notorious for this, because there is usually at least one contributor who sends their chapter many months after the deadline, thus holding up the whole book. While you should read all, or at least most, of the publications in the field, you cannot quote from it all; selectivity is essential. If there are too many papers to quote from, you can say, 'first demonstrated by Jones *et al.*, and recently reviewed by Smith'; or 'several studies have reported e.g. . . .' . As a general rule of thumb, if something is so accepted that it is in text books, you do not need to reference it, e.g. 'insulin stimulates glucose uptake' would not require a reference. Note that published data are normally described in the present tense (i.e. as a fact), while your data are normally past tense; e.g. 'NGF is neuroprotective' (Jones *et al.*), but 'the results presented here show that NGF was neuroprotective to PC12 cells'.

ACKNOWLEDGEMENTS

In addition to quoting published work of others, it is also good manners to name people who helped with the study but are not authors, and to thank funding bodies and any donations of reagents. Funding bodies usually *require* acknowledgement, and if reagents, cells or animals are provided free of charge by companies, but with a formal agreement in place, it will be necessary to obtain their written permission to publish the work (see Chapter 9). For a thesis, the acknowledgements go even further, because they inform the examiner of exactly what you have and have not done, and the wording can be important, e.g. 'Susan Jones provided technical assistance with some of the growth assays', is very different to 'Susan Jones performed the growth assays'. The second case means that you played no part in the measurements and cannot claim them as your own work. For papers, acknowledgements are usually brief and to the point, whereas in a thesis many students provide short, amusing anecdotes about the assistance they have received.

THE THESIS

Writing a thesis (for a Master's or Ph.D.) is likely to be the most difficult piece of written work most scientists complete. It is usually long, must bring together work conducted over several years (much of which probably did not go as planned), will probably be almost exclusively your own work and is conducted at a time when you have little experience of scientific writing.

The Ph.D. varies considerably in duration from three years in the UK and some other parts of Europe to six years or more in much of Scandinavia, and theses also vary in size and format. Many theses in Europe are now presented as a set of five or six published or submitted papers with relatively short introductions and conclusions. For this type of thesis, the research is demanding – five or six papers, mostly first author, is a great deal of work, but at least the writing is relatively easy. In contrast, in the UK the Ph.D. thesis is usually longer (200–400 pages), more detailed than published work, and often written when only a small part of the work is published. In the USA a Ph.D. is undertaken in several stages including about two years of course work with an exam, a written proposal within years 2–4 which is assessed and a final thesis at the end of the Ph.D. Writing such a tome is a daunting task for most young scientists, and this is where the choice of a good supervisor/mentor and a sympathetic lab pays off. They will be invaluable in helping you plan and write, and inevitably in checking and criticising what you have written.

Look through as many past theses as you can (particularly those that were most highly praised). From these you will see the types of style and format and the level of detail required. For example, the thesis can be presented as separate chapters of introduction, methods, results and discussion, or split into more chapters, each with shorter versions of these sections. You need to check local regulations then decide what is best for you. Are your findings better described as a single long series of interlinking experiments with an overall discussion at the end, or as a series of chapters each describing a set of experiments with their own brief introduction and discussion, followed by an overall summary and discussion at the end of the thesis?

When you are writing, think of your examiners. Hopefully your supervisor will select them (perhaps in discussion with you) as early as possible, because it may influence the way you write. They should be experienced, ideally eminent people who know your field, but who will also be sympathetic to the difficulties you may have encountered. If possible do not choose examiners who are known for being aggressive and argumentative, or are in direct conflict with your supervisor or your lab. Examiners are busy people, so do not assume that writing more will necessarily impress them, quite the opposite is true. Keep to the point and, if you have very detailed methods or numerous pages of primary data, they may be best located in an appendix.

As with all writing, try to lead the reader into and through what you have done. Thus, the introduction must provide both a general and specific background to the work. It usually helps to start off simply with the broad problem, but it is rarely necessary to cover the whole field in detail. The best introductions take the reader through the relevant status of the field, the problems and unresolved issues, leaving them with a feeling that they know what needs to be done next. Then, as they turn the page to see the aims of the work presented (which should be at the end of the introduction), they see laid out before them exactly what they had been thinking!

It is a most fortunate Ph.D. student who sets out with specific aims, addresses these in the time available and presents them in the chronological order in which the experiments were conducted. It is quite likely that the results of many months of hard work will fail to make it into the thesis. But they may be worth a few lines somewhere (perhaps in the general discussion), if only to let the examiner know about your great efforts and the time spent. There are some important differences between a thesis and a paper. A Ph.D. is a training exercise, and examiners recognise that not everything will have gone well, but like to see how you tackled problems and failures. So, unlike a paper, you may want to include experiments which showed that a technique was not appropriate, or that a hypothesis was incorrect. This allows you to discuss critically what was wrong. It is unfortunately very difficult to publish negative data in the scientific press. This can mean that erroneous or questionable findings remain accepted, as the literature is dominated by positive findings. In a thesis it is much more acceptable to present experiments which did not yield the predicted data.

As with any published document, great care must be taken on the final draft – check, recheck and then check again. Look at the literature just before the final version to make sure your work is really up to date. Make sure that each final copy is complete – photocopiers and printers sometimes 'lose pages' – and if possible print the examiners' copies on high-quality paper.

VIVA VOCE

The nature of the Ph.D. examination varies considerably between countries. In most there will be at least one internal (i.e. same university but distinct from the project) and one external examiner (e.g. UK), though in some countries there may be a panel of six or more, and in the USA and Germany the examiners are normally international. They will first read the thesis and determine if it is generally of the standard for a Ph.D. Then there will be an oral exam when the student is questioned by the examiners. In most countries this is a public examination which anyone can attend, though in the UK and USA normally only the student and examiners attend. Students may also be required to present a seminar on their work as part of the assessment. The nature of the viva depends not only on the country but also on the university, the examiners, the student and the thesis. Many of the same questions come up time and time again in oral examinations, e.g.:

1   Why did you choose this project?
2   What was the hardest/easiest/most enjoyable part?
3   How much help did you get?
4   If you had to do it again, what would you do differently?
5   What were the objectives, and were they achieved? What would you do next?
6   What was the most important/significant finding?
7   Can you explain any negative/contradictory results?
8   Can you explain the principles behind the methods/instruments you used? Are there better/alternative methods? How accurate/reliable were your measurements, and how did you standardise/calibrate them?
9   Can you explain the basis/reasons for using your statistical tests?

Are there better ones? How did you decide whether to present your data as tables, graphs or histograms?

10 Was the project/problem relevant to any particular aspect of basic biomedical knowledge, or does it have some applied/practical relevance (e.g. new treatments)?

Give simple, straightforward, uncomplicated answers; if the examiner wants more information/detail, let them ask, rather than run the risk of saying something stupid or incriminating. Listen carefully to the questions, and repeat them to yourself (out loud, if you like) before replying. If you are not sure what the question is, ask for it to be repeated, or rephrased. Do not be afraid to admit you do not know something, and do not be afraid to ask the examiner what their opinion/conclusion is. Keep an eye on the internal examiner – their expression can sometimes tell you when you are on the right/wrong track.

WRITING A PAPER

Even when your thesis passes the test, you must still get your work published in peer-reviewed journals, i.e. ones in which submitted manuscripts are assessed by two or more independent reviewers. Papers usually have several authors (see below), each of whom has contributed to the work and to the preparation of the manuscript – never submit a paper with someone's name included as an author without their permission and without giving them the opportunity to review the draft manuscript; whether they make any contribution to the final written paper is their choice.

The main criterion for publication is that you must have something new. An exception to this is when a major new finding has been published recently and requires confirmation, though even then it would be difficult to publish in a top journal without some additional information or confirmation in a different system. How you write the paper – the format, length and style – are dependent on what you wish to publish and on the journal to which you submit your paper.

WHICH JOURNAL?

The obvious answer to this question is of course the best journal possible – i.e. the most respected journal, which will reach the highest audience and will maximise the chances of your paper being quoted and your work seen. In your future search for jobs and funding, one, outstanding, first-author paper which is quoted widely, is more valuable than several multiple author papers (perhaps where your name is somewhere in the middle) in an obscure journal. The question of which are the best journals is a matter of considerable analysis, discussion and debate in the scientific community.

There is now wide use of 'impact factors' in assessing the value of scientific journals. These indicate the average number of citations per article in a given journal over the previous two years. Thus, it is believed widely that the higher the impact factor the better the journal. This assessment of citations is highly valuable, but has some pitfalls. Firstly, it favours fields and journals which publish rapidly. If new work is based on a published paper but it takes one or two years to complete it and publish the experiments, citation of the original paper after two years will not have an effect on the impact factor of the journal (as it is outside the period of analysis). This can be taken into account by data on 'half-life' which indicate *how long* articles are cited for. Thus, it is often most valuable to look at impact factors *within* a given field and to publish in the best journal in your field without worrying too much about how its impact factor compares with other areas of research. Journals which publish review articles often achieve higher impact factors, but may not necessarily include the best primary papers. In spite of these arguments, there is little disagreement that the 'high impact', interdisciplinary and most widely read journals are excellent (e.g. *Science* and *Nature*), and it is an aspiration of most scientists to publish in these. The problem with the very best journals is that acceptance depends not only on very good work, but also on its likely interest, which, in the case of journals like *Science* and *Nature*, means appealing to a broad readership. Certain areas of research which are highly topical and moving rapidly are more likely to be accepted in these journals.

In the very top journals, many papers will be rejected by the editors even without external review, on the basis of the general interest and impact of the work rather than the quality of the experiments. Therefore it is necessary to be realistic and practical about where to submit. Go for a good journal which is likely to be read by those in your field and which publishes high-quality work. Check how long they take to publish by comparing the submission date on the papers with the publication date. Here journals which publish, and ideally receive and review, electronically are usually much more rapid. Ensure that your work is appropriate in length (there is no point in submitting a long paper to a journal with a limit on the size of papers), and find out any costs of publication. Some journals make charges for publishing a paper, which are normally quite modest, but a few can demand significant costs for publishing, and many have high charges for colour prints. It is also useful to check the editorial board – does it include people who are likely to know your field and make a fair and informed judgement of your work? These considerations, and the final submission of the paper, will usually be undertaken by the senior author, but even as a student or young post-doc you should be involved in the process because at some stage the decision may be yours. As soon as possible, and with your supervisor's agreement, you should aim to act as the submitting/corresponding author on one of your papers. This means that the letter to the editor and all future correspondence with him/her will be from you, and your name will be on the front of the paper as the corresponding author. When submitting a paper it is necessary to include a covering letter stating that the findings have not been published previously (though presentations in abstract form are usually acceptable). It may be necessary at this stage (or later after acceptance) to assign copyright, i.e. all authors may need to sign a copyright form. Check that all aspects of format and presentation are appropriate for the journal and any disks included, describing the format – usually as a specified and commonly used word processing package or an ASCII file.

AUTHORSHIP

Deciding who is an author of a paper and in what order is often discussed only as the paper is in its final stages. This can be a tricky subject which is better considered and discussed openly as early as possible in the project. Authorship carries with it a responsibility and an assumption of intellectual input to the work. Thus, it has been argued that any author must have made a significant contribution to the conception, planning and design of the project; execution and/or the writing of the paper; and should understand and be able to defend all the work published. 'Honorary authorship', i.e. when authors are included simply because they are head of department, are involved in 'general supervision', they facilitated funding or allowed use of their equipment or lab, but had no direct involvement in the work, is not justified and should not be considered. However, the situation is not always so simple. A prerequisite of obtaining a valuable reagent may be inclusion of the donor as an author. A scientist or clinician who produces the essential samples for a piece of work will often expect authorship, and justifiably if she/he expends great efforts on preparing a valuable reagent which cannot be obtained elsewhere or produces clinical assessments and judgements. Another tricky case is over technical assistance – should the technician be an author or not? This case may be answered by considering whether they have simply performed routine assays or have developed and modified the technique. In other words have they done more than simply provide a service and have they contributed to the *science* (rather than the technical aspects) in the article? If not they should be in the acknowledgements rather than the list of authors. In practical terms, it is usually better to err on the side of caution and include authors (if they wish to be included) even if it is not fully justified. But remember this for the future, and when the time comes when you are invited to be an author, yet know that it is not really justified, you should offer to review the manuscript, but defer the offer of authorship, however tempting.

The practice of presenting authors alphabetically is now rare, but the order of citations is very important. The first author is usually the one who has done the work (most often the Ph.D. student or post-doc). The last author has normally overseen the work, obtained the funding and has co-ordinated the preparation of the work for publication. Authors in between have made more minor contributions. Problems can arise when two or more people have contributed equally to the work. It is possible to name them as joint first authors, but the one which actually appears at the beginning of the list always has the advantage. There may be a trade-off, e.g. one could be first author on one paper and the other on a later one. Decisions about such issues can be difficult, and should take place through open discussion, as early as possible and with the direction of the senior author if ill feelings are to be avoided.

THE EDITOR'S RESPONSE

When your paper has been submitted, try not to hassle the editor – you need him or her on your side. If you have not had a response in a reasonable period (this varies according to the journal, but a maximum six to eight weeks would be reasonable) a polite enquiry about the status of the paper is appropriate.

When the letter comes back from the editor, it will normally include detailed comments from several reviewers and the editor's overall decision. Acceptance (outright or with minor revision) is cause for celebration. More often the editor will use phrases such as 'may be acceptable' subject to revision (minor or major), perhaps involving 'further experiments', or it might be rejected outright. The first and most common response to what is felt as personal criticism is to believe that the referees were unfair, biased or did not understand (or even read) the paper. This may be true, but more usually they will have made some valuable points. Having read their comments, stop and reflect for a while – are they justified, have they discovered some major flaws and can you/should you address their views? Read the editor's letter very carefully. Phrases such as 'potentially acceptable after revision' or 'could be resubmitted if the referees concerns can be addressed', mean what they say, i.e. you must make major revisions and/or address each one of the comments in a detailed written response to be resubmitted with the revised paper. The phrase 'is not acceptable in its current form' may also allow resubmission, but 'rejection' or 'not acceptable' mean just what they say. In these cases it is rarely worth a lengthy debate unless you really feel that the reviewers' criticisms completely fail to recognise what is in the manuscript or their arguments are flawed – and you can back up your views with facts. Then it is often best to write to the editor addressing the concerns and politely requesting another reviewer – it may or may not work. Sometimes, mainly for highly competitive journals, there are no major criticisms, but the paper is not considered to have sufficient impact, general interest or novelty. Again, it can sometimes be worth entering a discussion with the editor (perhaps by phone) and some authors are more successful at this than others, otherwise choose another journal and try again, but take into account as many criticisms as possible – it could go to the same reviewers!

REFEREEING A PAPER

If you pursue a career in science, the time will come when you are sent manuscripts to review. This is an important and responsible task and one for which you should 'do-as-you-would-be-done-by', i.e. be as fair and unbiased as you hope your referees will be – even if the paper is from a competitor. If you cannot review the paper because of a conflict of interest (e.g. you have worked with the authors), you do not feel sufficiently expert to give a fair review or you do not have the time, send it back immediately. You should, wherever possible, complete the review (probably with advice from someone more experienced) and return it on time.

There is a tendency for those with little or no experience of reviewing manuscripts to spend an inordinate amount of time on this and to focus on fine detail. Like most activities, practice makes it easier and faster, but you have to begin somewhere. Ask to read manuscripts that your supervisor or a senior colleague is reviewing, then see how their comments accord with your views – at first they may not. It is helpful to the editor and the authors to structure your review into separate sections on major (i.e. those which cause most concern and require significant additions or revisions) and minor points (e.g. typographical, format or additional detail). Only in the confidential section to the editor should a view be given on whether the paper is acceptable or not. Keep a copy of your review, because the paper may come back to you after revision. Some journals ask one of the reviewers to write a brief article or editorial about the paper, to appear in the same issue. This summary should put the article you have reviewed in the broader context and usually in a way that is easily followed by the non-expert.

REVIEWS, ABSTRACTS AND OTHER PUBLICATIONS

Peer-reviewed papers are the publications that really count – ideally in good journals, with you as first or last author. You should always try for such a paper even if it means spending a little longer and conducting a few more experiments. At times that just is not possible and you certainly want to avoid long gaps in your CV. So, the smaller paper in a less-prestigious journal can be important, and abstracts resulting from presentations at meetings may be helpful very early in your career (and the talks or presentations are very important – see Chapter 6), but they should appear under a separate section, and later, as you have more papers, they will probably be omitted from your CV.

Reviews of the area in which you work can also be rewarding and help your career, but beware – they often take a great deal of time for rather little reward. A senior colleague may ask you to co-author a review and this will provide good experience. Such articles published in high profile journals, such as the *Annual Reviews* or the *Trends* journals, will probably be read and quoted widely, and often help in getting further invitations to write or speak. Chapters in books are likely to attract rather a narrow audience and can be very slow, particularly when the volume depends on multiple authors.

Other articles such as those in society newsletters, popular science magazines or even local publications at your institution will all help to raise your profile, but may take too much time. Be selective and decide how long you will have to spend before agreeing, rather than regretting it later as the deadline looms or failing to submit what you pursued. What really matters in research is primary papers.

FURTHER READING

See: http://www.cma.ca/mwc/uniform.htm for an excellent discussion of many aspects of preparing and submitting a paper and authorship.

Horton, R. and Smith, R. (1996). Time to redefine authorship. *British Medical Journal* **312**: 723.

Day R.A. (1989). *How to Write and Publish a Scientific Paper.* Cambridge: Cambridge University Press.

Davis M. (1997). *Scientific Papers and Presentations.* San Diego, CA: Academic Press.

On Being a Scientist (1996). Washington, DC: National Academy Press.

6

Communication and getting known

Scientific research is not complete until its results have been made known.

Only a speaker with nothing to say goes on and on as if he were laying a smoke screen.

The primary means of communication within and between the vast scientific community (and those outside science) is through publication – papers, reviews, books, general articles (see Chapter 5), but there is much more to it than just the written word. There are many forms of oral presentation – short and longer talks, poster presentations, personal interactions, group discussions and 'networking'. All of these are important (and becoming more so) for a successful scientific career and for getting known in the scientific community. Each one of these, whatever the size or composition of the audience, should be approached in the same way, taking time and effort to prepare a clear and professional (but not too flashy) presentation. As with writing, available technology – such as sophisticated graphics software and audio visual facilities – leave no room for excuses about sloppy presentation.

Few students or young scientists (and equally many older and experienced ones) have the natural flair and confidence to speak to a large audience, but practice, training and constructive criticism can turn even the most timid and mumbling speaker into a polished presenter. Most graduate training programmes now provide many opportunities for oral presentations – lab meetings, departmental or group sessions, posters and talks to a wider group in your university or research facility.

Learn everything you can from your senior colleagues – both the good and the bad points. There are many inexpensive, clear and excellent short books which provide advice on public speaking, preparing audio visual presentations and handling discussions (see Further reading). Take every opportunity to attend seminars and lectures by experienced speakers. There is a great tendency for busy scientists to skip many of these because the title does not sound so appealing, the subject is not directly within their area of interest or they simply do not have the time. It seems obvious that time should be made for scientific presentations of direct relevance to your own research, but it is also important to listen to those which may not seem so directly relevant, especially if it is an eminent and talented speaker. Not only does this broaden your understanding of the wider field, reveal new techniques and approaches and provide new ideas, in addition you may be (unknowingly) watching a future colleague, boss or reviewer of your grants and papers, and will learn a great deal about presentation.

PREPARATION AND PLANNING

Speaking to a large audience of eminent scientists can be a daunting prospect – and never worse than when you are ill-prepared. The first thing to determine (as far in advance as possible) is exactly what will be required. For a poster, what is the exact size and shape (landscape or portrait), are there specific instructions on layout and how long will you need to be with your poster? For a talk, who will your audience be – will it be general, comprising people with little or no knowledge of your field, or a more specialised group which may need less general background and more depth; will students be present? What facilities will be available; what is the time allocated? All too often speakers talk about *what they want to say* rather than thinking about *what the audience expects or wants*. It is inappropriate, and even annoying, to launch into a detailed discussion of your recent data, using technical jargon and describing sophisticated and complex techniques to a general audience, unfamiliar with the subject, without sufficient background and explanation. Scientists will usually be able to follow a talk in any field, but only if the terms and approaches are explained clearly, and if the work is put into context. Otherwise it will be incomprehensible, and, after all, why should they be interested if you cannot explain the relevance? All too often scientists (usually but not always, the less experienced) seem to feel that a talk packed with data, racing from one experiment to the next without pause, summary or explanation, will impress those listening. This view is mistaken. What will impress is a clear presentation which often has less data, but which introduces the background, aims and questions to be addressed, explains the basis of each experiment and what the results mean. This shows clear thinking, an appreciation of the subject, and, most importantly, an understanding of your audience.

Of equal importance is timing. Check very carefully the time allowed and whether this includes discussion. A twenty minute slot on a programme would normally mean a fifteen minute talk followed by five minutes of questions. *Never* run over time (see below). It is rude and unacceptable. Timing also needs practice and preparation, and while a minute or so deviation either way may be acceptable, talking for twenty-five minutes in a twenty minute slot which should include discussion will alienate the audience and the organisers, and may mean you are 'blacklisted' from further meetings.

Having established what is required, a plan of the talk can be made in the same way as for a paper or a series of experiments. Any talk should include an introduction, explaining the background (i.e. the scientific problem), the goals of the work, what was done and how (in most cases methods will be brief), the results and what they mean. Then practise as much as you think is necessary, particularly in front of colleagues who will be brutally honest in their criticisms. Make sure that the timing is right and you know what you are going to say. For the very inexperienced and nervous presenter, it can help to literally *learn* your first talks off by heart – but be careful that they do not *sound* learnt. Even for the experienced speaker, knowing what you will say in the first few minutes and the order of your slides or overheads is necessary. Strangely, although practice is important, for some people *over-practising* can be a problem, leading to a rather 'flat', final presentation. This is something you can judge only by experience. Many seasoned speakers will have worked out what they will say, but do better not to practise formally. Until you have experience, err on the side of caution – better the 'flat presentation' than a complete silence part way through, as you completely forget what you were going to say next.

POSTER PRESENTATIONS

It is now common at local, national and international meetings to present research findings as posters, i.e. presentation of your project, methods, results and conclusion on a large (usually about one metre square) poster displayed on a board for the audience to view and discuss with the presenter. Once the format has been checked, the content and layout need to be decided. Do not cram in too much – posters should be simple and clear, and able to be read at a distance of one metre. The best posters include a large and clear title, a summary of what has been done, simple graphics and/or tables with self-explanatory legends and a set of conclusions, often with bullet points. Keep the written text to a minimum and in large font – most senior scientists will be short-sighted and short of time. Avoid glorious technicolour – a few complementary (usually primary) colours looks classy and clear, but too many colours are distracting. Numerous shades of pink, lavender, orange and lime green are horrible. Most research institutions have the facilities to produce large posters on single glossy sheets, which look professional, are easy to carry and need less pins or sticky tape (which are always in limited supply at meetings). This format also allows you to print off small sheets of your poster which can be handed out to people at the meeting; they are extremely helpful and may get you remembered later.

Check the times when you are needed to attend your poster and *stay by it* (barring brief calls of nature or medical emergencies). Remember that just as you nip off to have a chat to your friends, the most eminent scientist will inevitably pop by and you will miss them. As you stand by the poster, smile politely and tell anyone who stops by that you would be happy to answer any questions they have. This makes them realise that you are the poster presenter and gives them a chance to ask you about the work, or move on to the next poster. Do not pounce on people. There is nothing worse than the over-zealous student trying to monopolise your time with the minute details of their experiments when there are fifty more posters to see. Most visitors to posters will be interested and polite. Occasionally the questions will be really tough. Do not bluff. Instead admit what you do not know, and if necessary say that you are rather new to the field and that your supervisor may be able to help them (supervisors, or at least a senior member of the lab, should always accompany students to their early poster presentations).

At some meetings you will be bombarded with visitors and questions for several hours, but at others hardly anyone will come by and none may stop to ask questions. This should not be taken as a reflection of the quality of your work or dishearten you. It is common and usually reflects the type of meeting, the interests of the attendees and what else is going on at the time. Posters are an excellent way of presenting and talking about your work in small groups or in a one-to-one setting. They also allow detailed discussion, but are unlikely to get the wide exposure afforded by a seminar or platform presentation at a large meeting.

ORAL PRESENTATIONS

With good preparation and planning, and advice from as many people as are willing to listen to you speaking, even presentations to large (and seemingly frightening) audiences can be enormously enjoyable and rewarding. The first time can be a literally sickening experience, when your heart is pounding, your legs feel like jelly and your mind is a complete blank. Even very experienced speakers and eminent scientists are usually a little nervous before a talk. This is normal, and when a speaker is not at least slightly nervous, the presentation is usually not so good. I know a Nobel Prize winner who, after a career of about fifty years and hundreds of presentations, is still almost unable to speak to colleagues before a talk because he is so nervous. Young speakers always have the sympathy of the audience and the chairman – they expect you to be nervous and even to make some mistakes. In order to minimise problems, check out the venue well in advance. It may look large and daunting, but in reality it is no different to a small room. Make sure you know exactly how to control the lights and audio-visual system, determine where the pointer is and, if it is a laser, which end to point at the screen (not the audience), and who your chairman will be. If possible have a brief word with the chairman beforehand, and if it is your first presentation, let them know – they will be sympathetic.

The first sentence of the presentation is the hardest, so make sure your know it by heart and have *brief* notes to remind you of what is next. But *never* read a presentation, and remember that you may not be able to see your notes when the lights go down. Detailed scribble on numerous cards will also be impossible to follow when you get going. If you really forget what to say, stop and take a deep breath, then carry on – most people will not notice, those who do will understand. Beware of laser pointers – a minor hand tremor becomes an enormous movement when projected on to a large screen twenty feet away (so hold with two hands balanced on the podium and use only when essential). Never waiver the pointer about all over the screen, point clearly to what you want to illustrate, then turn it off. During a talk, face the audience as much as possible, make eye contact, but if possible not with a single person – you might just intimidate them. Choose a number of spots and people in the audience to focus on at different times. Check each slide as it comes up and as you talk through it – it could just be the wrong one. When nervous there is always a tendency to rush or even gabble – try to keep stopping for just a second, and take a breath. Always keep your head up and talk to the back of the audience. Do not be nervous about taking a short break and a gulp of water if you need it.

Good manners and humility are essential in oral presentations, particularly for the less experienced. If you miss a slide or find one upside down, apologise then carry on. Underplay rather than exaggerate your data – unless you want to attract aggressive questions. Perhaps most important of all, try to sound as though you are enjoying yourself (even if you would rather be almost anywhere else) and that you are *interested* in your results. If you sound bored and monotonic, how can you expect your audience to stay alert and awake? Let the audience know that you are enthusiastic and interested but also critical of the data. At the end always say thank you, then nod at your chairman and the projectionist.

QUESTIONS

As you breathe a sigh of relief at the end of your talk, do not relax too much – the questions are still to come. They are usually benign, but there is a danger that as the adrenaline subsides, you will completely miss the question. Listen carefully to the questions, never interrupt, and if you do not understand what the questioner is asking, request that they clarify. Answers should be brief and to the point – *do not ramble*. However, aggressive, rude or inappropriate the questions may seem, you must *always be polite* and calm. This is not always easy, but *do not rise to the bait* of an aggressive questioner. If the discussion gets into a detailed or prolonged exchange, it may be best to offer to discuss this in more detail after the talk. This is rare, particularly for young scientists, and any good chairman would intervene. It is common to be asked about something which you presented very clearly in your talk – the enquirer may have just missed it or have been asleep. Most of the rest of the audience will be aware of this so do not try to be clever by saying that you 'did include' what is being asked or even suggest that the enquirer missed the point – just answer the question as though you made no previous reference to the issue. This will gain much more respect. Try not to smile like a Cheshire cat when someone compliments you on your presentation. It may be followed by 'However…', and the devastating criticism. When the questioning is over, smile and walk off quietly – leave the pointer behind and do not forget to collect your slides. One of the most embarrassing things I have seen was a young presenter who rushed off the stage in relief at the end of her talk, taking the podium with her as she had forgotten to take off the neck microphone. If possible, stay around during the next sessions or breaks in case someone wants to ask further questions, rather than running off to the pub to celebrate or drown your sorrows.

At some stage, in some talk, somewhere, things will inevitably go wrong or interrupt you. People will arrive late, the chairman will introduce you with the wrong title, the projector will break down or the computer crash. Stay calm – the audience will be very sympathetic. If the projector or computer fails, wait for just a minute or so then suggest that you carry on and do so as best you can without the audio-visual facility. This is much better than an embarrassed silence for ten minutes. When projection facilities return do not go through everything all over again, but summarise only the essential points. Be prepared to give a brief summary of your talk without slides or overheads, often it can be better than when the talk is 'cluttered' with data! This gives an impression that you are professional and in control. Meetings are carefully timed and anything which holds them up (especially speakers who run over time, whether their fault or not) cause disruption and annoyance.

AUDIO-VISUAL AIDS

It would be most unusual nowadays to give an oral presentation without some sort of audio-visual accompaniment, and presentation of data is almost impossible without some sort of projection facilities. The first decision to be made is what type – overheads, slides (single or double projection), PowerPoint or even black- or white-board drawings? The choice depends on what facilities are available (always check in advance), the size and type of presentation and how you feel most comfortable. For teaching purposes, or in a small informal setting, black- or white-board illustrations or drawings on an overhead projector made during the talk can be most appropriate, but these techniques do not work so well in a large auditorium or at a formal meeting, and depend to some extent on your artistic abilities (though some of the best talks I have seen were given using a black-board when the speaker's slides were lost or forgotten). Prepared overhead sheets (transparencies) are preferred by some, and are particularly favoured in less formal settings. The disadvantages are that the projection may not be so clear, they can stick together or you may drop them on the floor. The advantages are that you can see exactly what is coming next and they are cheap, quick and easy to prepare. Transparencies can be very professionally produced and many of the potential problems can be avoided by keeping them in plastic folders in a ring binder. This form of aid is often preferred by industry and also means that you are more able to modify at the last minute – most places have facilities to quickly print out new transparencies. You can also delete or add overheads just before or even during your talk, for example if you need to add or delete something in light of earlier speakers, or if time is running short. Once your slides are on the projector (and in a large meeting, are usually outside your control), such changes cannot be made.

The ability to adapt to the situation, to save time or avoid repetition is a sign of the accomplished and professional speaker.

Slides or electronic (usually PowerPoint) presentations are used most commonly, particularly in large venues. PowerPoint presentations have many advantages – they can also be modified at the last minute, allow some very impressive graphics and videos to be included and avoid the need to carry large packets of slides around with you. There are also pitfalls – computers can crash, files get corrupted and some places do not have the necessary facilities. It can be useful to take your own lap-top computer so that you are familiar with the system (but ensure that the connections are compatible). In countries overseas, the computer software is likely to be in the native language – Japanese is, for English speakers, particularly difficult to guess, and the commands and keyboards are not identical across the world. When you feel confident to use electronic presentations, back-up slides may still be reassuring – at least for a while.

For slides, check them several days in advance – it is difficult (and expensive) to get new ones made at short notice. Invest in a slide wallet and take a few slide covers with you. All too often the glass covers crack in transit and look horrible when projected. Clean them just before they go into the projector. If you are going to present in a large room, check how your slides look from the back of a similar sized room. If this is not possible, anyone with reasonable vision should be able to read a slide at arms length without projection. If they are not clearly legible – change them. On slides, use a minimum of text or data in a large and clear font. On the front (white) side of the slide-cover place a dot in the bottom left-hand corner. This is standard format and is used to orientate the slide when it goes into the projector. For most projectors (e.g. carousel) the slides go in upside down and back to front, so that the dot can be seen on the top right-hand side from behind the slide when it is in the carousel. Once your slides are loaded before your talk, check through all, or as many as possible in a projector; most large meetings have facilities for this. Determine if you or someone else will control the projector (or computer), and never be rude to the projectionist.

Double projection can be used effectively to illustrate a presentation, particularly in a large theatre, but it is not a means of showing twice as many slides! This can also go horribly wrong when (as frequently happens) the two sets of slides get out of synchrony and both you and the projectionist become confused. An important rule of thumb for presentations (which is most important for the less experienced) is to *keep them simple*. Scientists tend to be rather conservative and are not often impressed by flashy graphics unless they are essential to the talk. There is nothing worse than trying to be really clever in a presentation, only to find that it all goes wrong. The same is true of the content of slides or transparencies. You simply cannot use extensive, small text, tables with numerous columns or detailed or complex figures and diagrams, and expect that your audience will follow or even read then. It is very annoying to see a slide projected and be told by the speaker that he or she knows you cannot read it or tells you ignore half of it. The audience is left wondering why they bothered to show it at all. Do not simply read from the text shown on a slide. For each slide, use clear headings which state the point, clearly labelled symbols and histograms. As each slide goes up take a few moments to explain it to the audience. It is helpful to go through the format quite carefully on one of the early slides, then explain that each of the following slides will follow the same format. When you have talked about a series of experiments, summarise them with a brief slide. It is useful to do this at several stages during the talk. This helps the audience to keep track, and may regain the attention of those who have started thinking about something else or fallen asleep. At the end have a simple concluding slide, then of course the acknowledgements – your collaborators, supervisor and the funding body. If you have been invited and paid to speak always thank (verbally) the organisers, then later a brief note or email of thanks afterwards is also much appreciated.

BORONS

Whilst there are many excellent books and papers on the subject of scientific presentations, one of the best and most enjoyable discussions of this subject by Peter Medawar's *Advice to a Young Scientist*. He emphasises the importance of judging your audience, of keeping them interested and attentive, and pitching your talk at the right level. An excellent piece of advice that Medawar gives is to try talking to nine-year old children – when they are interested they stare at you in fascination, when they are bored they fidget within about a minute – learn to judge adult audiences in the same way. Medawar describes 'borons' as the people who drone on to an uninterested audience exceeding the allotted time. To him this is one of the most serious errors a scientist can make. 'There is incidentally no more expeditious way of making a life-long enemy than to poach upon the next speaker's ration of time – something that should never happen anyway if the chairman is awake.'

MEETINGS

Attending and speaking at scientific meetings is an essential part of scientific life. It can be hard work and time consuming, but also great fun. You meet interesting people and travel to exciting places – and you should get good feedback. The many and varied types of meetings serve different purposes. National meetings are important to get to know scientists in your own country. You may meet your future Ph.D. examiner, grant assessor, peer reviewer or employer. Large, international meetings, sometimes with many thousands of scientists, can be very exciting, but quite daunting. They are one of the best ways to see top speakers reviewing the field and to present your work as a poster or a talk. They can also provide an excellent opportunity to make contacts and look for jobs – many large meetings have 'job fairs' or 'employment services' where you can be interviewed on site. At meetings of this size, selectivity, planning what you want to see in advance, and time management are essential – lecture theatres may be ten minutes or more apart and there can be literally thousands of posters. The most rewarding meetings are often those which are smaller, with perhaps just about a hundred participants, but more focussed in your area of interest. They are often arranged so that all participants meet, eat and stay together or are in close proximity, and provide an excellent way to talk to colleagues and follow up on their (and your) presentations.

Attendance at meetings is expensive – travel, accommodation and registration costs all add up, even with special rates for students. If you are lucky, your grant or fellowship may include travel costs, or your supervisor will have adequate funds, but more usually you need to get some independent support. There are many sources of such funds, though eligibility varies. Some are specifically for students, while others exclude them, and almost all require that you are presenting your own work. Searching around for funds long before you even plan to go to a meeting is worthwhile and sometimes essential because deadlines for applying for funds may be long before the meeting you hope to attend. Many national and international societies provide travel bursaries, but often require membership for a year or so before applications will be considered. Since student subscriptions to such societies are usually cheap, check them all to see which provide travel awards, then join. If you really want to go to a meeting and money is tight, there are lots of ways of cutting costs. Most meetings offer very inexpensive student accommodation and room sharing. Be inventive and imaginative, and you will get there.

NETWORKING

Getting known and respected within the scientific community is very important for future success, and meetings provide an excellent opportunity for this. Clear name badges and good eyesight are important in order to spot who you want to speak to, and attendance at their talk is essential. Ideally a senior colleague or supervisor may introduce you to the eminent scientists you have always been longing to meet, but this does not always work out and it is difficult to simply walk up and introduce yourself, particularly as the senior scientist will have no idea who you are. If they do know your supervisor and she/he is not at the meeting, you can always use the excuse of passing on their best wishes to the person you want to meet. You can try to stop them and ask a question following their talk and hopefully they will have the time to talk to you – and even remember you in the future. Do not be disheartened if senior scientists seem brusque or disinterested; they are busy and may simply have other things on their minds. But, in general, scientists are very happy to talk to enthusiastic young people and are helpful and friendly. Coffee and tea breaks, poster sessions and dinners, or evenings in the bar are where most of the real scientific discussions take place. Make sure you are around, and try to avoid the temptation to go off with your friends – you may miss an important opportunity. If you do talk to someone about your work, you can always follow it up with a note later, maybe with a reprint of your paper, or a short email saying what a pleasure it was to meet them. Do not expect a reply, but provided you are not too pushy, your name is more likely to stick in their memory.

If meetings are organised by someone you know well or are held at your home institution, the opportunities for talking to attendees are much better. Helping busy, older scientists to find where they want to go, track down their lost luggage or make reservations and enquiries for them will almost certainly be remembered favourably in the future.

HOSTING AND CHAIRING

Hosting meetings or senior speakers, and chairing sessions are activities that most scientists will have to undertake at some time in their careers. Graduate students and young post-docs may be asked to host senior speakers, or even chair presentations, particularly at local meetings.

Organising a seminar and a visiting scientist requires some forethought. It is important to give the visitor all the information they will need well in advance – timings, audience size and composition, accommodation. Offer to help with travel (e.g. you can check train times and meet them at the station), and ask if they have dietary preferences (it is wise not to present a vegetarian with ham sandwiches), and who they would like to see. They may not reply until rather late before the visit – successful scientists are sometimes disorganised as well as busy. It may be better to find out if they have a secretary and make arrangements through him or her. Once details of travel and arrival and departure times are agreed, arrangements for discussions with staff and students, the venue for the talk, meals, etc. can be planned. Attention to detail is important, but the most important thing is to ensure that there is a good audience for the seminar and plenty of discussion. It is very embarrassing to invite an eminent scientist then to find only five or six people in the audience. Talk to the speaker before the presentation to get a few details for your introduction, show them the room, audio-visual arrangements (with a spare projector and batteries for the laser pointer if possible) and check that she/he is happy to answer questions – inevitably they will be, but it is polite to check. You may be required to entertain the speaker before and/or after the talk. It is a good idea to invite one or two others along. Ensure that reimbursement for expenses is dealt with, and after the visit send a note of thanks.

Chairing a pre-organised session at a meeting requires rather less preparation, but still involves responsibilities. Check out the room so that you can help the speaker with the microphone, pointer, lighting and audio-visual controls. Make sure you can pronounce the speakers' names and the title correctly and, for multi-author presentations, that you know who is presenting. Read the abstract well in advance, and of course listen to their talk carefully. If no one in the audience wants to ask a question, it is the responsibility of the chairman to do so.

Keeping to time can be a tricky task. This is the chairman's responsibility, but of course you do not want to be rude to the speaker. It is advisable to state at the beginning of the session the time allocated to each talk and discussion, and the need for speakers to keep to this. It is usually necessary to allow a minute or two run over, but then if you are away from the podium you can move up towards the speaker in the hope that they will take the hint. If necessary, ask them if they might summarise because time is short. If they do run over seriously, the chairman is in a difficult position, but a polite statement such as 'I am very sorry but we are going to have to move on very soon due to the time constraints', will be necessary. Then you are justified in shortening the discussion time. After the talk, thank the speaker and invite questions, trying to keep your eye on

the whole auditorium and on who asked what. If questions are not
audible, summarise them briefly. If the discussion gets into prolonged
debate with a single questioner, suggest that perhaps it could be continued after the session. When all speakers have finished, thank them again.
Professionalism and preparation are the key tactics.

FURTHER READING

Medawar, P.B. (1979). *Advice to a Young Scientist.* Basic Books.
Davis, M. (1997). *Scientific Papers and Presentations.* San Diego, CA.: Academic Press.
The world of post-docs (1999). *Science* **285** (several articles).
Fischer, B.A. and Zigmond, M.J. (1999). Attending professional meetings success-
    fully. http://www.pitt.edu/#survival/attend.html

7

Moving up

Synergism is the key word in collaboration.

WHAT CAREER?

Completion of a research degree usually takes several years, considerable hardship and very hard work (but hopefully also enjoyment and reward), yet in research this is just the first step on the ladder. Addressing the question of what career may seem unusual and even depressing after spending so long in research training, but it is practical and necessary. Within research there are a number of ultimate career paths – academia (ideally a tenure-track or tenured, faculty position), research institute or industry. It is often too early to make that decision at, or even soon after, completion of a Ph.D., but a view on your ultimate (and realistic) ambition is helpful. It would be unfair and untrue to say that all (or even most) Ph.D. students achieve the goal of a career in full-time research. Such positions are highly competitive and relatively few compared to the number of successful Ph.D.s. Many who choose to undertake a Ph.D., do so with uncertainty about what they want to do. For some it is simply a way of putting off a decision. But even those who undertake a Ph.D. with a burning ambition to secure a life-long position in research may eventually do something else which they had not planned, either through choice or necessity. This can be viewed as failure and a waste of extensive training, but this is a rather negative and even naïve view. Experience in research and acquisition of the numerous skills involved in this activity is enormously valuable for a range of challenging careers, and puts research-trained scientists at the forefront of many career opportunities. A research degree is a waste of time only if you have really disliked the research – which is why it is better to get out as early as possible (ideally after completing your degree) if it is clear that this is not something you enjoy.

The choices in science are numerous, but sometimes tough, and often they are not made easily or most effectively just before or after completion of a Ph.D. All too often the next step has to be made quite early during research training, long before you have the real experience to make an informed decision. But hopefully you will have seen a little of the good and the not-so-good about research. Research towards a Ph.D. is necessarily focussed, and in some countries the very short time for Ph.D. studies (e.g. three years in the UK) leaves little or no opportunity to undertake really exciting and risky work. There is considerable pressure to complete experiments, present your work, get papers published and submit a Ph.D. thesis. This pressure will not go away, it is a basic fact of research. But at least in future you should be more prepared, and rather less constrained. Unless you are quite talented and somewhat lucky with your project and supervisor, research for a Ph.D. generally allows rather little scope for independence and individuality. Thus, the real pleasures of research – having your own ideas and carrying them out yourself – may not be fully realised. Because the decision about whether to embark on a research career or to choose other avenues is difficult to make so early, many choose to do a 'post-doc', which can (hopefully) allow you to achieve some independence and give you time to make decisions and to see the good and the bad side of research.

POST-DOCTORAL POSITIONS

The traditional 'post-doc' position is funded (usually through a grant to a senior scientist) for a variable period of one to five years. Timing is important – if possible avoid a short-term position of anything less than two years unless you are assured of further funding or it is really just a stop-gap for a specific project. Few research projects can be completed successfully in less than two years. This can (and should) provide the opportunity for a young scientist to really prove and establish themselves, to gain new experience and expertise and to take an important step up the ladder to scientific independence. It can also, unfortunately, be the graveyard for some young scientists.

Choosing the right post-doc position (like any other career step) depends on careful thought and informed advice, on your own ambitions and aspirations and on a certain amount of luck. The same criteria apply as those already described for deciding on a Ph.D. place (Chapter 2), but, for a post-doc, you also need to ensure that you will have the opportunity, encouragement and necessary support to become independent and to achieve the markers necessary to move to the next step in your career. A post-doc position, unlike a Ph.D., does not have such a defined end point. For the former, it is in the interests of the supervisor to ensure that the student successfully completes a thesis and is awarded their higher degree. It is not always so simple for a post-doc. There are some (hopefully rather few) supervisors who use post-docs as work-horses to simply 'get the work done', with little concern for the career or primary goals of the young post-doc. It is therefore very important to investigate the views of your potential lab head, and find out how their previous post-docs have fared in their careers.

There is now great concern by governments and funding bodies about the fate of 'contract research staff' who are made up almost exclusively of post-docs on short-term contracts. Such positions are usually a stepping-stone to something else, which provide valuable training and allow development of independence. However, like all research, such achievements may be slow, the temptations to stay on in yet another post-doc position in the same lab are great, and personal constraints often make a major job change difficult. Several countries and institutes are now trying to address the career structures for young scientists, to bring in better working conditions and provide regular advice, but this is slow.

It is important to stay in touch with your ultimate career aims, to continually check whether these are realistic and achievable, whether you are going in the right direction and whether your supervisor shares your own views and goals. Many institutions have brought in formal mentor schemes with regular meetings (independently of your immediate boss) to monitor your progress and goals, and post-doc career development and training programmes. If these are not in place, you should encourage your institution to bring them in, or you will be forever dependent on your supervisor/mentor or on sympathetic colleagues. Use anyone who is experienced to help as much as you can. If your busy supervisor only wants to discuss results and experimental plans, ask for a formal meeting to discuss your career. If this turns out to be not as productive as you might have hoped, ask a senior member of staff if they could help – but approach this carefully by saying that you would value advice from someone independent; they may be close friends with your supervisor. In either case, prepare for the meeting by providing your CV and trying to identify your career aims, options and ambitions.

A post-doc position is the normal step after a Ph.D. Many young scientists will move into a second post-doc, in the same or a different lab; but, if this happens, think carefully. The scientific world has many 'career post-docs', who move from one short-term contract to another, some-times into middle-age, with little or no security. It is a very sad fact that there are few positions (at least in the academic sector) for the talented 'bench scientist'. In research institutes and industry such staff are (quite rightly) highly valued and respected – it is they who conduct the vast majority of the research, and their expertise and experimental skills are highly valued and respected. In universities, the situation is somewhat different. Research is funded largely on the basis of rather short-term, externally funded grants, which provides rather little security for the post-doc. Success in academia is, perhaps unfortunately, based largely on group leaders and independent scientists rather than the essential staff who actually conduct the research.

There are two possible views of this situation. Firstly, the real concern is that so many talented young staff have little or no job security and for many little prospect of a real career within basic research. An alternative view is that in many well-funded labs, security for post-docs is as good or better than in many other careers, and that those who enjoy their work, and are willing to remain on externally funded projects, should not be discouraged. These are complex issues. The practicality is that external funding of academic research is unlikely to change for the foreseeable future, but such institutes can and should provide training and advice to young post-docs. They must ensure that this group is collec-tively and individually aware of their options – the opportunities and the pitfalls. The decisions can then be made on an informed basis by each individual. In practical terms, if you are really happy as a post-doc and not concerned about security, then why not carry on? However, for those with different career aspirations, with financial and social commitments which may require rather greater security, or who are unhappy with their position, alternatives must be sought.

MOVING – PLACES, PROJECTS

Great emphasis is now placed on varied experiences in science – varia-tions in lab, projects, techniques, location and collaborations. This often means that a period in another lab, another country and on another project will help your career. A breadth of experience benefits most careers (and indeed many aspects of life) and should be sought, and, where possible, seized. The first post-doc position may be in an environ-ment, and on a project you know – the second position, whether as a post-doc, a fellowship, or in a more senior appointment, should ideally include a varied experience. However, such moves are not always possible or optional. Social factors often influence geographical moves (see Chapter 13) and some young scientists may be working in the very best (or even the only) lab in the world in their field. If this is the case, it is important to try to demonstrate additional experience, through short contracts or interactions with other labs (if possible abroad), developing collaborations with leading scientists overseas and broadening experience.

Changing your project at a stage beyond Ph.D. may seem tough. Indeed one of the reasons many young scientists say they do not want to take up positions in industry is the concern that they may enter the company to work on a project related to their experience, but will be moved into a completely different area of research. This view is naïve and rather negative. If you work on important problems, the specific area does not really matter and if you are a good scientist the specific project does not matter. You will of course have built up a great wealth of knowledge and experimental expertise in your own area, and changing projects means learning a whole new background and technical approaches. But in fact this takes much less time than might be imagined, and the challenges, excitement and insight of entering a new field can more than balance the fear of something new. This does not mean that you can skip frequently from area to area. As a young scientist this will not help your curriculum vitae, but carefully planned changes, which (ideally) move into more challenging and realistic areas of research are often very beneficial. Usually such changes in direction are forced by external pressures (e.g. job availability), but at best they are driven by personal choice.

FELLOWSHIPS

Personal fellowships provide independent funding (usually including your own salary) for you to undertake the research of your choice, usually where and with whom you want, and are also an important step in your career towards independence. They are prestigious and indicate the quality of your research and scientific ability, and show that you can attract independent funding. All these factors are extremely important in undertaking a research career.

Further details on writing fellowship applications are provided later (Chapter 9), but the first step is to determine if this is what you want and can achieve. Most young fellowship holders will have a sponsor or mentor to help them along, but the assumption is that a fellowship will allow you to make the important and exciting, but quite demanding, transition to independence. The ideas and choice for the project, the direction of projects and supervision of staff will ultimately be your responsibility, and you must of course have a real passion for research.

The competition for independent fellowships is high and depends on your research achievements (i.e. your CV), on the quality of your planned project and on the choice of institution and sponsor. Selecting the right fellowship which is appropriate to your experience and career stage is important, as is the location, lab, mentor and, most importantly, the research project.

ACADEMIC POSITIONS

Most scientists will have some research experience in universities. Those few who leave after their first degree and conduct a research degree in an independent institute or in industry may have more limited experience but they should have at least some knowledge of what university life is like. This means that they should recognise the numerous and conflicting demands on the time and effort of university staff, the need to continually secure funding for their research and produce high-quality papers, while supervising and teaching students, organising and examining courses, and meeting the ever-growing demands of administrative duties. Those with no experience of university life tend to think that the 'academic' enjoys the luxury of flexible hours, limited teaching and several months holiday over the summer months when the students are away. How far this is from the truth! Recent surveys of university life in the UK and USA suggest that most academic staff work well over fifty hours a week and many have a much more gruelling schedule. Nevertheless, this is a very fulfilling job with the freedom to change your research project as you wish (provided you can obtain external funding), and with great opportunities for innovation, imagination and personal satisfaction.

Career structures in universities vary slightly around the world, but in general follow a similar pattern. The first appointment is usually at lecturer or associate professor level. In the USA these are rarely tenured, but may be 'tenure-tracked', i.e. with the expectation of a tenured position, subject to satisfactory performance, usually in both teaching and research. Progression in the USA can then be through assistant professor to full professor – beyond that a chair appointment would normally mean a head of department position. In some US (and other) universities, even a full professor position may not carry tenure, and continued employment depends on research activity and securing external grants, which may also be required to pay part or all of your salary. In the UK, first lectureship positions (unless defined as temporary) frequently have a contract until retirement age, provided that a period of probation is undertaken satisfactorily (usually three years). Promotion may then be to senior lecturer and reader (believed to be the equivalent of US professorship). A chair (with the title of professor) can be an institutional position (e.g. as head of department), but may also be awarded to an individual (personal chair). Other countries have systems not so dissimilar to these. Faculty positions are offered in open competition to candidates who can demonstrate the best track record and potential, largely in research but also in teaching. However, in some parts of Europe, appointment to faculty positions still has vestiges of 'who you know' rather than how good you are, but this is changing, albeit slowly. Germany has a slightly different system, where, after a long undergraduate training, Ph.D., then standard post-doc, scientists aim for an 'assistant's' position. In order to obtain this it is necessary to achieve the 'habilitation'. This is a rigorous assessment of the candidates' track record in research (usually publications) and teaching, and may require at least a decade of research. Here again, there are moves to change the formal habilitation and replace it with a system closer to that in the US and UK. Japan's academic system is somewhat like that in Germany where scientists would hope to progress through post-doc to joshya (a senior post-doc), and jokyoju (assistant professor). There are still very few post-doc positions in Japan and association with a senior scientist (professor) is important, if not essential for success.

Salaries, promotion prospects, teaching and administrative duties, lab space, etc. vary enormously, not just between countries, but between institutions and departments. It is usual to negotiate a 'start-up package' when offered a university position. This can include discussions on salary, position and contract, lab space and funds to set up a lab. Wealthy research-active universities can offer very attractive start-up funding, and in the US such packages are generally much higher than in Europe (though rarely include tenure). Not surprisingly, the more senior the position and the more a university wants to appoint you, the better the offer is likely to be. This can be negotiated to some extent (again, more so in the US), but it is unwise to make unrealistic requests. Try to find out what recent appointees of similar experience have secured, and what the university can realistically afford and provide. In the UK, unreasonable demands and hard or protracted negotiations are not a good start to a new job in a place where you may be working for the next twenty years or more.

RESEARCH INSTITUTIONS

Many positions in research institutions are short term or non-tenured, i.e. they are potentially renewable subject to performance, usually at five-yearly intervals, but may carry no guarantee of security. Some do offer fully tenured positions with the opportunity for career progression and the advantage of considerable resources. Research institutions across the world have outstanding reputations, e.g. Howard Hughes Institutes in the USA, Max Planck in Germany, CNRS and INSERM in France (where a large proportion of research in France is conducted), Karolinska in Sweden, EMBL in Germany, Medical Research Council units in the UK and many smaller private and public institutions across the world. Although there are the many attractions of research institutes (not least their strong research reputation and funding), the opportunities for such positions are quite rare and very competitive. Some scientists prefer the academic environment of universities, with a broad range of subjects and greater opportunities to teach, while others prefer the environment of industry.

RESEARCH IN INDUSTRY

To those without direct experience of working with or within the commercial sector, the attraction of such positions is often the resources for research, the salary and of course the potential for fringe benefits, such as company cars and business class travel. Undoubtedly, these are strong incentives (particularly given the rather low level of salaries for most academic positions and the likelihood of debts caused from student life), but industry has much more to offer.

Research in industry can be highly varied – between companies, large and small, traditional multi-nationals and small start-ups, and within them, and depending on whether you are working at the discovery stage, validation or development/testing. The biomedical sector of industry is vibrant, but changing. On the plus side, the research is thriving, new biotech companies are starting up all the time, great opportunities are offered by information from genome sequencing and there are many major diseases which are untreated. On the less positive side, security is not always so good, particularly in the smaller companies where funding can be uncertain, or, as a result of mergers of companies, projects can be 'killed off' quite suddenly (even when the research seems to be going very well) for a variety of reasons outside the scientists' control or even understanding, such as market forces, competitors and the need to prioritise projects.

There has been a tendency for academic scientists to 'look down' on commercial research, believing that it offers less opportunity for freedom and for creativity. This view is most commonly held by those who have little real experience of industry and have failed to see and feel the excitement of drug discovery, or of seeing an idea, a piece of research and many years of hard work actually culminating in something of real practical benefit. The approaches, expectations and demands within industry are somewhat different to those in academia. Research in a commercial organisation is directed towards different goals – identification of a target or a product is the key goal, team working is critical, deadlines are often very tight and flexibility is essential.

The choice of a research career in academia or industry is not easy and may be determined largely by opportunity and circumstance, but, like all decisions, the choice should be made only when as much information, experience and advice as possible has been gathered. Researchers can enter industry at many stages – after first degree or Ph.D., after completing post-doctoral studies or as a senior scientist with an established reputation. However, while many move from academia into industry, the reverse is rather uncommon. This may of course reflect real contentment of scientists in industry, but a move back to academia is also associated with an inevitable cut in salary. Another factor is research output. Academic positions usually depend on continued, high-quality publications and an ability to attract external funding – neither of which can be generated easily in industry. Within some companies (particularly the smaller ones) there is a strong culture to publish, and academic institutes recognise that scientists wishing to return to academia from industry may have very different CVs. Nevertheless, it is worth remembering that if you enter the commercial sector it is certainly not impossible to return to academia – but it is quite unlikely that you will do so.

OTHER CAREERS

Whether by necessity or choice, many scientists leave research, sometimes after many years. Some step into career paths in related subjects, such as publishing, teaching, research funding, administration, licensing or marketing of scientific products or legislative issues such as patents. Others leave the world of science altogether for areas such as finance, public relations, politics and even the arts. Such a career move, even if forced by circumstance, should not be viewed negatively – otherwise you will never be happy. Nor should the years spent in research be considered a 'waste of time'. The benefits, skills, experience and attitudes gained from research are considerably greater than are immediately realised. This is why scientists, if trained well, have excellent job prospects. They have (or should have) learnt to think logically, to plan and review, to work in teams, to deal with problems, to present themselves and their work in oral and written form, and they will also of course have good skills in other key areas, such as computing, speed-reading, summarising, prioritising and much more.

Deciding to leave research – perhaps after spending a long time in a somewhat cosseted environment – can be stressful and difficult. Most universities now offer advice and training on alternative careers, with opportunities to meet people who have taken a similar 'big step' and who are usually only too happy to help and advise. Senior colleagues are also likely to have contacts who will talk to you about the pros and cons of various careers. Your colleagues, mentors and senior staff in research may view your departure from science as something of a failure – at least on their part. Scientists train scientists and hope to create others 'in their own image'. Therefore the fact that they have failed to attract you to their beloved profession (particularly if you have done well) often leads to disappointment. In reflecting on over twenty Ph.D. students I have trained, I know this feeling only too well – but then I remember that those who pursued careers outside research all now earn considerably more than I do and seem perfectly happy!

CURRICULUM VITAE

A CV is much more than a few pages which you dust-off and brush-up whenever you are seeking a new job or position. It reflects who you are and what you have achieved. Nice presentation and snappy statements on a CV may help a little (and a scruffy, out-of-date and poorly prepared CV can be highly damaging), but really it is what you have achieved that is important. Unless you really can find no advice and are very poor at presenting yourself, money paid to groups who 'optimise CVs' is rarely worth it – it is the content that matters – though scientific colleagues can advise on how to make your CV look significantly better.

Gaining experience, achievements and recognition is a process which needs to be worked on. The important aspects of your CV will undoubtedly depend on the position you are seeking. For a post in industry, some experience in, or collaboration with, companies is a great help, for a job in scientific journalism it is essential to have shown an ability to write, and for a job which involves extensive teaching you must have shown you can and want to teach. Similarly for research, output is the key factor. In science this is predominantly publications (see Chapter 5), though other 'esteem factors' – particularly those that demonstrate you are (or can be) independent – are moving up and being recognised by your peers are also important.

Ideally you will have a number of first or senior author papers in good journals. While quality is OK, long gaps between publications (particularly recently) are a problem, which at the very least you will need to explain. Combining peer-reviewed papers in the same list as reviews and abstracts may seem to boost your CV, but it is annoying to the reader who is likely to want only to see the real papers. Keep them separate and list papers chronologically (and in full) rather than alphabetically. It may help to star key papers, note the discoveries they describe and your contribution, particularly if this is significant, e.g. 'I instigated this work, conducted 50% of the experiments and wrote the paper . . .' or 'the first author is a student which I supervised directly, I also directed most of the experiments . . .'. It is particularly important to note joint, first-author papers or ones where you are not first or senior author for a good reason, but made a major contribution to the work. Good reviews are important, abstracts are barely worth mentioning. Some people quote the impact factors of the journals in which they have published, which is probably not that helpful. It is the work rather than the journal which matters, and, if it is a good journal, people will know that. The only exception might be a somewhat obscure journal, which has a higher than expected impact factor. Citations of your work can and should be quoted but only if they are high (certainly greater than 50).

It is usually worthwhile putting your discoveries into a descriptive context. Unless a lengthy descriptive section is requested, keep your whole CV as brief as possible. A one page summary of what you have done can be helpful. Try to summarise your experience and achievements, perhaps under bullet points but always say what you have achieved not what you have done. For example, avoid 'I studied . . . using . . . approaches', instead say 'I used . . . to show that . . .', 'My research revealed . . .', 'I discovered . . .'. A section on future research goals is also important. Some prospective employers may require quite a detailed research plan. If they do not ask specifically for this, include just a page or two of the major directions, hypotheses and how you will achieve them – but be realistic!

It is not usually appropriate to include details of school or pre-university education once you are at or beyond Ph.D. The first degree you obtained (the classification, year and university) are important as are any prizes or special awards. Critical reviewers will look not only at these, but also at what you have worked on and who with. To have worked with a recognised world leader is important, as is of course their support as a referee. Select the most eminent referees you can, who you are sure will be sympathetic. Contact them well in advance (to ensure that they are happy to act as a referee), give them the details of the post you are applying for and send your current CV.

Most other aspects of your CV relate to evidence of your independence/recognition or to specific experiences relevant to the job on offer. The latter may include techniques you have used, knowledge of a particular field, activities such as teaching, supervision, writing, managing research or equipment, etc., depending on the job. Here you need to try to look into what the advert and job details are asking for (and perhaps even telephone the contact person), then highlight these on your CV. Do not despair though if a job specifies certain experience or techniques that you do not have – many prospective employers will still take someone who overall looks like they have promise rather than exactly the right background.

Independence and recognition are rather harder to achieve, but often quite easy to spot for someone reading your CV. Good papers are the prime consideration here. As a young scientist you may have several excellent first author papers, but the question will be whether you were just a good lab worker in the right place at the right time. Measures of independence and recognition could be prizes and awards (apply for any you can), invited presentations, particularly at international meetings (here accept any invitations even if you are a substitute for your supervisor), and external funding. At the early stages in your career, invited presentations may be only seminars at other universities (but it is important to say that you were *invited*). Any funding obtained, even small amounts, are important initially. Later in your career, significant external funding will be expected (see Chapter 9), and it is then important to state if you are the principal investigator and name any co-applicants, together with the source, amount and duration of funding and the type of project.

Additional information on a CV needs to be considered carefully. It is important to explain justifiable career breaks (e.g. for family reasons or illness) and other activities, such as time out on another career. In general for other aspects list only achievements not activities. So for example do not say you enjoy sport, writing and music, but do say if you were a first-team player, you had articles published or have given public performances as a musician. These all show your abilities and diversity. Say if you have been a driving force behind things such as journal clubs, new teaching or graduate education or changes in policy.

For most academic positions, teaching is very important. You need to show experience (as much as possible) and interest. Having done some teaching is important, but better if you can say that you organised a course or initiated a new tutorial programme, and if available give assessment scores (unless they are poor).

NETWORKING

'Networking' was discussed earlier, but its importance cannot be understated at any stage in your career, perhaps even more so as you are moving up. This is the time when you will be submitting papers and grant applications, receiving invitations to meetings, establishing collaborations and seeking referees and support. Networking does not mean selling yourself against your principles (which actually can be detrimental), but it does mean taking time in getting to know the people in your field in your own country and overseas, particularly by attending and giving talks at meetings. Your real value will be assessed from your published work, but everyone remembers an excellent speaker, someone who took time to help or support another scientist or student or who was a valued collaborator. They remember even more the person who accepted an invitation but pulled out at the last minute, who failed to return papers or grant applications to review or reneged on agreed collaboration. Enemies can be made easily – often unintentionally or unjustifiably, and sometimes irreversibly. Avoid this if you can – make friends, establish productive collaborations and treat everyone without prejudice. Joining national and international societies, and participating in their activities, helps you to get known and build collaborations. Taking on responsibilities (e.g. secretary/treasurer of societies, organiser of sessions, etc.) will gain respect, but be careful because they can take up huge amounts of time. Invitations to join editorial boards, society activities, grant committees all carry responsibility and have benefits, but reflect carefully, and if you cannot meet the demands, decline politely.

INTERVIEWS

Sitting in front of a panel of senior staff, often revered experts in their field, defending and trying to promote yourself against a barrage of clever and sometimes sneaky questions, while desperately wiping sweaty palms, can be a horrific experience – recalled by many as the 'job interview' or the 'promotion panel'. The first thing to remember is that they have all been in your position. A few seem to have selective amnesia or take delight in belittling young scientists (mark them down for the future!), but most are sympathetic and helpful. They have to ask penetrating and sometimes uncomfortable questions, but they are not out to 'get you' and usually want very much to help you. It is most unusual to find an interview committee which is really set against you and trying to be difficult – unless you come across as being cocky and arrogant or, on the other hand, they think you are superb and really want to challenge you.

A great difficulty faced by interviewees is to achieve the balance between enthusiasm and promoting what you have done, against the downside of appearing arrogant and lacking self criticism. This may vary between jobs, interview committees and countries. Self promotion and confidence are probably valued more in the USA than in some European countries. In the latter an almost self deprecating, apologetic presentation of achievements and in your reactions have been normal in the past. But things are changing and the international scene is getting more balanced.

Many analyses have been performed on interviews – on how the candidate should present themselves, look, talk, respond and behave in general. Science, we like to think, is above the normal prejudices, but in reality interview committees are all made up of humans with their own views and failings. Thus, we have to take note of the fact that interview committees tend to form a strong opinion within the first few minutes of the interview starting. These opinions (whether right or wrong) can be difficult to change.

I hope (and believe) that in science, what you wear and how you look, your gender, racial background, spoken accent and any disability have little or no consequence compared to your real attributes and abilities relevant to the subject. But it is impossible to say that perceived character does not influence the opinion of interviewers. The committee needs to believe that you have not only ability, but also the confidence and drive to succeed. One of the best ways to learn how to perform in an interview is to serve on interview committees – an opportunity which is only rarely presented to young scientists. The next best is to take all the advice you can get.

Planning for an interview is essential. Find out exactly what is expected of you, how long it will last and if possible seek out everything you can about the interview committee – who they are and what they do. Interviews are normally extended events, not simply the forty to sixty minutes facing a committee. For established positions in academia or industry, they may even span several days. There may be a 'pre-interview' visit, which is useful to get to know the people and the place. Every aspect of this will be important, even the informal times such as lunches and dinners. On each occasion you will be making an impression and opinions will be formed, even if the setting seems very relaxed (NB do not drink too much alcohol at such events). Because faculty positions may involve teaching, your presentation skills will be important and will be critically assessed in the interview and probably in a research seminar, and you maybe asked to present a short lecture at a level for undergraduate students. Discuss all of these with a trusted, senior colleague – plan, prepare and practise. As with any talk, do not assume that more is better – interview committees may include staff who are not experts in your field and they will not be impressed if they cannot understand your presentation or if you run over time.

For industrial positions, the interview process can be complex and testing. It may include 'team activities' with other applicants, general problem solving, comprehension tests and acting out difficult situations. Key attributes for most companies are not simply abilities within a specific scientific field (which you almost certainly have if you have got that far), but also include flexibility, imagination, team working and the ability to identify and achieve ever-changing goals. Such interviews may seem tough, and, if you fail, it may simply reflect intense competition or your inexperience – but it may also indicate that you are not really cut out for such a career.

Questions in interviews can be many, varied and sometimes completely unexpected. It is likely that you will be asked why you want the job and what you will bring to it, what are your career aspirations over the next five and ten years, what do you see as your major strengths and weaknesses, how will you fit into the organisation and meet its needs, what are your immediate plans for research and for seeking funding? Be sure that if there are weaknesses in your CV (e.g. a lean period of publications or an earlier poor exam result) you will be asked about them. As far as possible be honest and recognise the weaknesses, but give an acceptable explanation and say how you have moved on. Some of the trickiest questions are the ones intended to see how you can 'think on your feet', but for which there is no right or wrong answer – the panel may just want to see how you respond. Examples of this are numerous and can range from: 'Do you feel that reviewers on papers and grants should be named?' or 'How much time should you devote to really high risk research?' to 'Should young faculty members be free of teaching for several years or teach immediately?' and 'Do you think its better to have predominantly graduate students or post-docs in your lab?'. There are many acceptable answers and no real right or wrong ones. You must show that you have an understanding of the question, a balanced view and an ability to give an opinion on the spot.

Never lose your temper or raise your voice in an interview in response to even the most aggressive questions. Sometimes this line of questioning is simply to test your commitment, patience and self confidence – always be polite. Rarely, you may be asked a completely unreasonable and unexpected question (e.g. of a personal nature). If this arises say that you really feel it is not appropriate to answer this – but nevertheless if you can then do so – even if the question is unfair. I once saw a female candidate asked about her commitment to a position in view of her young family. The question was immediately waived by the chairman who deemed it completely inappropriate and unacceptable. The candidate then said that she also felt it was inappropriate but nevertheless chose to answer very positively, won enormous respect from the whole committee, and got the job. However, you should never be asked such questions and there is no obligation to respond.

Always be brief – there is nothing worse than an interviewee rambling on, and this is a real danger when you are nervous. If you do not understand a question, say so and ask for further explanation. Avoid criticising your potential future employer unless it is done very politely (and very constructively) or if you really do not want the job, even then word travels fast. At the end of the interview you may be invited to ask questions. Keep these to a minimum. Try to sort out your major questions beforehand, and those of less importance can be asked in less formal settings or you can save them until later if you get an offer. Importantly do not mess people about by going to interviews for jobs you really do not want, failing to make a decision on an offer long after the agreed time or bringing up late and increasingly demanding requests – science can be a small world. If you fail in an interview most senior staff will respond positively to a polite letter thanking them for the opportunity and invitation, saying how much you enjoyed meeting them and politely asking for any feedback they can give on reasons for your failure which may help you in the future. Finally, try to have confidence in your abilities, be natural, enjoy yourself as much as possible and learn from every interview – particularly the really bad ones.

FURTHER READING

Fisher, B.A. and Zigmond, M.J. (1999.) Attending professional meetings successfully. hhtp://www.pitt.edu/~survival/attend.html

Davis, M. (1997). *Scientific Papers and Presentations*. San Diego, CA: Academic Press.

The world of post-docs (1999). *Science* **285** (several articles).

On Being a Scientist (1996). Washington, DC: National Academy Press.

8

Responsibilities

Most scientists are young in years .... No one actively involved in research thinks of himself [or herself] as old.

Securing the job you had been aiming for – perhaps an academic post in a University or a scientific position in a research institute or a company – brings a great sense of achievement and relief. It also brings new responsibilities, exciting challenges and significant changes in your working life. It is likely that you will have the sole, or at least the major, responsibility for the direction of research in your lab and of all those working with you, securing funding, managing finance, publishing and writing reports.

DIRECTING RESEARCH

In theory, if you have secured an independent position, you will probably have been successfully directing your own research for some time. In reality, it is likely that you will have done this with regular advice from the lab head or other senior staff. It can be a little frightening to realise that you are now the lab head (even if it is a very small lab at first), who makes the decisions and is responsible for the successes and failures. There is a temptation to totally 'go it alone' and stand or fall on your own abilities. A few will do this very well and achieve great success, but most young scientists will benefit from continued advice. Indeed some of the most successful senior and experienced scientists seek the advice of respected colleagues on their draft papers or grant applications, on ideas, project plans and results throughout their career. You may remain in contact with your previous mentor or talk regularly to senior colleagues in your new environment. Seek out those who you respect as scientists, who have proven success, and are keen to help younger staff.

The transition to an independent position and to leading your own research might lead to conflict with your previous boss. If you worked on a project in his/her lab which originated and which will continue there, it may be difficult for you to continue the work in your new position. Continuation may depend on reagents from your old lab. Even if you feel that a project is 'yours' (i.e. you started it and worked on it) it is necessary to discuss this with the head of the lab you are leaving. She/he may have grants to continue the work and other staff working in the same area. Such issues can often be resolved amicably so that you each take a complementary rather than competitive line, reagents are shared openly and collaboration continues. There is almost always more than enough for two groups to do. Try to avoid setting up in direct competition (and conflict) with your ex-boss – she/he will normally be in the stronger position and could (even without serious ill-intent) hold back your future career. Most difficult situations can be resolved by a little thought and by give and take.

Do not be too ambitious when you first start. Stick to a good project on which you have a track record, which is likely to attract funding and to yield results. This does not always coincide with the most important and ambitious aspects of research. In an ideal world you would always try to work on 'big' and important projects, since these are the only ones that are likely to yield really important results (unless you are remarkably lucky and happen to stumble on a major finding). But a balance is needed. You will probably have to put in two or three grant applications and set up several related projects (but do not get tempted to diversify too much initially). Some of these should be addressing major and difficult questions which may take a long time to produce results, but they can be balanced by projects which can be set up more quickly with a high chance of yielding publishable (but less-important) data. The latter help you to keep publishing, gain confidence and can be important for student projects. Initially your publications may come from an earlier post-doc position with your previous boss as senior author. As soon as possible you need to publish work from your own lab, with your own funding. It is not unusual for this to take several years, but the sooner the better.

The major failings of young scientists first directing their own projects are over-enthusiasm, over-ambition, unrealistic expectations of projects and approaches which are extremely difficult and not very practical. It always feels as though your project will work, the results will be complete within a few months and the paper ready to submit soon after. This is rarely the case, particularly when you have to set up your lab and techniques, you have less time to conduct the research yourself, need to train others and to meet many demands on your time. As you move up the career ladder you will depend more and more on others in your lab, on their contributions and drive and on your ability to get the most out of them.

MANAGING PEOPLE

If you have chosen to work in industry, your task of 'people management' is likely to be a little easier. You will be trained and advised, regularly assessed and have a clear structure for management, detailed information on actions to be taken and sources of advice. In universities, the situation is much more flexible and a little haphazard. Some universities run courses on personnel management, but they are often given by managers rather than scientists. The young academic therefore tends to rely on advice they can get from senior colleagues and, all too often, by learning the hard way.

Numerous books have been written on managing people. These tend to be dismissed by scientists who have little time or interest in such issues. In fact they can be quite illuminating and helpful and provide some simple pieces of advice on dealing with people. For example, always listen, then think before you act, try to put yourself into the other person's shoes, criticise how they have behaved, but do not criticise them personally. To say, 'you seem to have behaved rather unfairly', allows room for improvement, whereas to say, 'you have been unfair', is likely to be taken personally. Try to come to conclusions together (ask them if you think your account of a problem is fair or not) and where possible let them rather than you identify the cause of the problem. Dealing with people is one of the trickiest things a boss or leader in any field has to do. Everyone is different and responds differently to each situation. We have personal expectations of how they should behave, but of course the person you are talking to may have a completely different experience and view.

Most successful scientists lead by example and enthusiasm. We have the great advantage that the people we supervise want to be there – if they do not, show them the door! This makes management so much easier. You can try to suggest rather than dictate and encourage rather than demand. Leading by example is not always easy though. Younger scientists will not always see the whole picture. They may question why they are hard at work in the lab, while you seem to be always at your desk, on the phone, or flying to exotic places, seemingly enjoying yourself. Think back to when you were a Ph.D. student and did not really understand what your supervisor was doing and why they were away, and try to take time to bring your group into your activities. This does not mean justifying everything you do, simply explaining.

A considerable difficulty for the young scientist is the direction and management of post-docs. You are barely different from them in age or experience, want to be their friends, to socialise and participate in their activities, yet you also have to direct what they do, and sometimes perhaps to reprimand their actions or lack of activity. Respect is of course earned, not imposed, and leadership is best achieved by example. This means that as a lab head you must be fairer, work harder and be more careful in the way you handle people than ever before. There will be people who work with you that you like or dislike for personal reasons. But you cannot show this, though it is of course acceptable to praise those who put in greater effort.

One of the most important qualities in a research leader is real enthusiasm for research. Scientists are not noted for their strong interpersonal skills, are often absent-minded about the people around them or completely oblivious to their personal problems (in part because they are so excited and driven by their subject). Enthusiasm is infectious and tends to drive and support those around you. Different staff need different types of supervision and support. Technical staff usually appreciate more specific direction, together with regular feed-back and involvement in the overall direction of the project (though some are able to direct, assess and present projects with considerably more skill than the post-docs). Graduate students require training (see below) whereas post-docs should be (though often are not) heading toward independence, developing their own ideas and supervising others. Some individuals may need space and to work independently, some want reassurance, others respond only to encouragement while others need deadlines and occasional reprimands. Many of the potential problems of managing staff can be limited by selecting and appointing the right people in the first place.

APPOINTING STAFF

The best labs will receive numerous, unsolicited communications from bright young scientists wishing to work with them, and sometimes even bringing their own money. For less well-known labs and those starting-up, recruiting good people is much more difficult – particularly if you require specific skills or the post is for quite a short period.

Advertisements in major journals and on web sites (and here it helps to have a good web site of your own with some details of your lab and its research) may result in many applications but not necessarily of high quality. All too often the majority of applicants will not have a strong research record, do not have the relevant skills, or are from overseas and it may not be possible to meet and interview them, or even determine if they can speak English fluently.

The best way to recruit is through personal interaction and direct contact with other good labs, not just when you have a post available (though you should then email appropriate colleagues), but well in advance. Always be on the look out for bright young students and post-docs who may be seeking a position in the future – even if it is likely to be a year or so in advance. The best place to see such people are at meetings. Make a note of excellent presentations or posters and talk to the present-ers about their future plans. Seminar visits can also help to identify bright young people and may offer a better opportunity for discussion. Ask senior scientists whom you respect (for the training they provide as well as for their science) about who may be coming through their lab and looking for a position in the future.

When you do get applications, check them out carefully and always seek references. Ensure that the referee knows the candidate well and is in an appropriate position to judge their scientific abilities (e.g. an ex-school teacher's reference may be helpful only in discovering the appli-cant's character, but not their abilities in research). Because of concerns about litigation, hardly anyone writes a really bad reference these days. Beware therefore of what referees *do not* say and check out comments of potential concern such as, 'Smith could do well in the right environment' (which implies he has not done well so far), 'Jones works best alone' (he does not get on with people), 'Davies works better with direct supervision' (do not trust him, he cannot work alone). Such comments can be com-pletely innocent, and it is important to think carefully when you are asked to provide references – the potential employer will be trying to read between the lines. Statements such as 'very good' and 'works hard' do not reveal much, 'competent' or 'average' amount to criticism. You should be looking for comments such as, 'outstanding', 'one of the best students I have supervised', 'in the top 5% of post-docs in my lab' (but check how many students and post-docs the person has had). The strength of a refer-ence is partly dependent on the status of the referee. For a world leader to say that a student is truly outstanding probably means they are a super-star. When someone says the same thing but has only had two students it does not mean quite as much. If in doubt telephone the referee. They are much more likely to be open on the phone. When you request references, ask specific questions such as, 'please comment on the applicant's technical and scientific ability, his/her ability to work independently, to work with others, etc.'. If the referee fails to respond to these specific questions it may mean that they are not able to say anything favourable. Another approach is to provide a set of boxes and ask the referee to grade (e.g. 1 poor to 5 outstanding, or bottom 10 or 50% top 50 or 10%) the applicant in a number of areas.

INTERVIEWS

In the end you have to interview the short-listed applicants. This takes time but is worth the effort. Applicants should have a formal interview, and informal discussions with yourself, other members of your lab and ideally with one or two other senior staff. With excellent applicants you may have to 'sell' them the position, so a planned visit involving meetings with enthusiastic and positive people and some social activities is important.

For formal interviews, ask one or two colleagues, ideally with experience and proven skills in appointing to join you. In most institutions, it is now essential to complete a short training course in appointment and selection before you can serve on an interview committee. The major reason for this is to ensure that you are fully aware of the laws on equal opportunities, fair assessment and appointment. These are often quite complex and rigorous, and you will probably need to establish requirements or specifications for the 'person' and the 'post', and make a formal note (to be kept on file) of why any candidate rejected did not meet the requirements. Formal recruitment courses can also be very valuable and considerably improve your skills in interviewing and selecting the best candidates.

NEW STAFF

When anyone new comes into the lab, it is important to spend some time with them and ascertain that they understand what is expected of them and what they should expect of you. Lay down the ground rules at the beginning. You will need to give them some time to settle in and get to know the lab and the people. Ensure they are introduced to everyone, and know what each person does. Get them going on their research project as soon as possible. Discuss their project and plans at the outset. It can be helpful to keep a file of plans and discussions, to be regularly checked and updated. It can act as a reminder of agreed actions, deadlines and prior-ities, and is a useful *aide memoire* for later discussions, which is particu-larly helpful if problems arise.

For technical and other support staff, working hours and holidays are normally fixed by the institution and quite formally adhered to. For research staff and students, it is much more flexible. You should let them know what you reasonably expect – are there general hours of working for the lab or times when they should be there, are they likely to have to work late into the evening or weekends? For most scientists the answer to these questions will of course be 'yes – as and when you need to in order to get your research done'. They may not be aware of this though. The new Ph.D. student may (unfortunately) not have thought about the fact that he will have to come in every day of the week to check his experiments, or that his/her experiments may be twenty hours long. They should also be clear about meetings and seminars they need to attend, reports, general lab duties, supervision and other activities that will be expected of them, and how often they should expect to see you.

SUPERVISING GRADUATE STUDENTS

Graduate students need special attention. Good supervision takes time and effort and has many frustrations, but can also be very rewarding and enjoyable. A Ph.D. supervisor is expected to train their students in practi-cal aspects of science (i.e. doing experiments), scientific method and initiative, experimental design, analysis and assessment, how to read, write and talk about science, and to work with and supervise others. You should also try to enthuse them about science, help them make career decisions, publish and present their work, and, in the end, turn in a high-quality thesis, on time. If this were not enough, the supervisor may also provide a shoulder to cry on, a friend, and an object of fear and hatred. In reality, and if you have chosen students well, most of these tasks will come naturally and easily. Your student will enjoy (most of) his or her research, will obtain interesting and publishable data (on which you will probably be the senior author) and go on to a successful career. Indeed of the many students I have supervised, there are none that I regretted taking on, in spite of a few headaches along the way.

One of the biggest enemies of the Ph.D. student is time – it just seems to slip away. It is therefore important to set the scene early on and always keep an eye on the ticking clock. Ensure that students know what is expected of them, then get them going on experiments as soon as pos-sible – even if the experiments do not work or are reproducing the work of others, there is nothing like getting a result in the first week to inspire enthusiasm.

Institutions normally now run extensive (and usually obligatory) courses for graduate students in everything from designing experiments and data analysis to scientific writing and presenting, collaboration and fraud. This can take a significant load off the supervisor, but rarely substitutes for one-to-one discussions, or putting such skills into practice. Get the student to talk and write about what they are doing as soon as possible. Within a few weeks of starting they should be able to present the plan of their project and how they are going to tackle it at a lab meeting. Rather than simply asking them to read around the subject of their project, get them to write a literature review for a defined deadline within the first few months. This should form a good basis for a later report, paper or thesis. Ensure that all data are analysed and well presented, and experiments are written up in a way that will make writing the paper easy. Students are notoriously disorganised. They may not file and document information well, forget meetings and fail to meet deadlines. Even if you as a supervisor are almost as bad, try to ensure that they get out of these habits. Challenge them as much as possible in every discussion and meeting. This can be done kindly and politely, but if they do not naturally think carefully about what they read, write and do, they need to be pushed to do so.

In the initial stages of a Ph.D., most of the ideas, organisation, critique and assessment will be done by the supervisor. This will and must change with time. Sometimes it is easier and quicker to tell a student what to do in an experiment, interpret the data for them and write the paper yourself. But this is no help to them. Ask what *they* think they should do and how, then let them try, even if it is against your better judgement (and at the risk of a costly experiment which fails). Sometimes they may be right, or will learn an important lesson.

Responsibility is an excellent way of stimulating young scientists. As soon as a student is ready, ask them to supervise an undergraduate student, give a talk or co-author a review with you. Towards the end of their Ph.D. they should be working more as a collaborator with you than as a student, directing most of what they do and telling you about the latest findings in their field and what they mean. Of course not all Ph.D. students mature in this way, and compromises need to be made. On occasion it becomes clear that a student really is not cut out to do a Ph.D. either because of lack of interest or ability. This is a tough situation for the student and the supervisor (particularly if it is one of your first students). Ph.D. students should be assessed regularly, by staff independent of the supervisor, for example at the end of each year. In this case, problems should be identified early on and involve discussion with other senior staff. Sometimes the student and supervisor simply do not get on, and one or both want a change of project and supervisor. Hopefully this will be possible and can be worked amicably with the help of other staff in the department, and should be learnt from. However, if problems arise with a Ph.D. student, and such a transfer is not possible, one option then is to appoint a joint supervisor – someone who is experienced in Ph.D. student supervision and can hopefully see both points of view and help to achieve a reasonable (if not always happy) conclusion. Regular meetings will need to be set up to monitor progress with everyone present. If you are a new or inexperienced member of staff you should have a joint supervisor for your first Ph.D. students and should consult with them regularly and take their advice. As a supervisor, you will also need to consider and discuss (earlier than imagined) the career options for your student, ensure that their thesis is completed on time and arrange the exam.

EXAMINING PH.D. STUDENTS

The examination of your first Ph.D. student is likely to be as stressful for you as it is for the student. It will get better with experience. But anyone who has put time and effort (and usually some sweat and tears) into their students will find the examination a little tense. Choosing the examiners is an important responsibility which needs to be considered carefully, in discussion with the student. Avoid inexperienced staff, direct competitors or those known to be aggressive and difficult. That does not mean selecting someone who is 'easy' or 'ones who just owe you', which is not fair on the student – even though they will protest that it is. In the end, most students want their final Ph.D. exam to be challenging, with a real in-depth discussion of their work – otherwise it is something of a let down.

The time will come for almost every scientist (especially those in academia) to examine a Ph.D. themselves. The format for such exams varies widely from a private discussion between a couple of examiners and the student in one country, to a public examination, in front of an audience of several hundred (sometimes in very formal dress) in another. Sometimes it is a foregone conclusion if the student has satisfied the written requirements, on other rare occasions it can be a gruelling ordeal resulting in complete failure. The latter may be almost as stressful to the examiner as to the student, particularly if it is one of your first.

Consider carefully before you agree to examine a student, and if possible agree only if you know the lab and the supervisor and believe that their research is of high quality. Ideally you will have seen the student present their work or read their paper. In this way you can avoid the really dreadful thesis which may fail. When you receive a thesis, considerable time will need to be spent reading it. It represents several years of hard work by the student and deserves more than a cursory glance by the examiner on the train. If, when you have read the thesis, you really do think that it is so poor that you will not be able to pass it, seek the advice of a senior colleague. If they agree with you, it may be better to return the thesis with a written report and say that the oral examination should not proceed. There is no need to put everyone through the trauma. The thesis may be resubmitted later – if you are lucky with a different examiner.

The oral examination, whether public or private, should ideally be an in-depth and positive discussion of the field, the methods used and findings of the student. If you believe that the thesis is of a high standard, tell the student, but you still need to be satisfied that they did the work, understand it and can discuss it. Avoid spending time talking about minor typographical errors. These can be listed in advance, handed out and corrected. They are usually trivial, unless errors are so common that the thesis needs to be rewritten before the student is examined. The focus of the exam should be the science. If you are asked to examine an overseas student – check what is the required format. In some countries it seems as though the examiner is the one being assessed because they have to present a resume of the work on the thesis and discuss it in front of a large audience, including not only faculty staff and students, but also the friends and family of the student. A good way to limit aggressive questioning!

APPRAISAL AND ASSESSMENT

A good supervisor/boss will be continually thinking about how their staff are doing and giving feedback on an informal and regular basis. Formal assessment and appraisal are also valuable and now required in most jobs. The two are quite different. The primary purpose of *appraisal* is for the career development of the person being appraised. It should be a discussion about how they can move forward and what they need for their development, but may include some actual evaluation on what they are doing well and not so well. *Assessment* is more normally applied to consideration for promotion and is a more obvious, critical evaluation of progress.

PROBLEMS WITH PEOPLE

When a group of people work together in the same environment each have their own aspirations, views, concerns and frustrations, so problems can arise. This is particularly so when these people are under pressure (e.g. to complete a Ph.D. or a paper, get a grant or a job) and ambitious. The lab head is the one who has to try to spot the problems as soon as they arise, assess where the difficulties lie and deal with them efficiently. There is no room for prejudice and favouritism or for ducking out, and it is necessary to keep your ear very close to the ground.

Problems may arise because a few people do not get on together; someone is simply not working hard enough, is sloppy, aggressive or gossips; or there may be prejudices or ill feelings, sometimes well founded, on other occasions they arise with no obvious grounding. Whatever the case (and it can be difficult to determine the root causes) everyone will feel that it is someone else's fault. First try to assess the facts. See the person or people separately and say what you are concerned about, then *ask them* for their views (even if you believe they are in the wrong it is only fair to hear them). Do not tell them what you think the core of the problem is, see what they think. If you believe that their behaviour is a problem, ask them if they think that they might have been unreasonable, rather than telling them that you believe they were at fault. Getting them to recognise and accept the cause(s) of the problem is a big step forwards. If this does not go as planned, suggest that others perceive they may have been difficult and see if they think that this is fair (hopefully they will see some reason). When this line of questioning fails, ask them to go away and think about it and come back to you, make them realise that, whatever the case, the problem has to be, and will be solved. If it is serious (e.g. major disagreements, potential harassment or even prejudice) involve another member of staff and possibly the personnel department. Sometimes it is better not to target individuals but to address the lab as a whole. For example, tell them that you are aware of frictions, gossip or disagreements, have a good idea of the causes and it must stop; this may limit the problem. Eventually, with serious difficulties, a formal reprimand may be required. Before doing so, take advice and ensure that you are acting correctly, follow necessary procedures and document everything carefully.

MANAGING THE LAB

The heart of any lab is the people in it, but there are other aspects to be overseen, organised and managed, and unless or until you are fortunate enough to have a senior technician or lab manager, this job is down to the lab head. It is necessary to ensure that the equipment is working and serviced, reagents are stocked, regulations (e.g. for health and safety, genetic manipulation, use of animals or human tissue) are adhered to and records kept, staff contracts are issued, students registered and much more. Most of this does not take up too much time, at least in a small lab, and students or post-docs can help, but even better is to find support from experienced technical and secretarial staff. Check who in your institution has responsibilities (and therefore experience) for these issues – they are important.

Managing the money is an important but often tedious task. Those who trained in well-funded labs rarely think about the cost of experiments – which can come as rather a shock when they have their own lab and find that the annual consumables budget is spent in the first three months. It is in fact good training for graduate students and post-docs to cost their experiments and budget for them accordingly. Later, as they take on financial responsibility, they will have learned to check accounts regularly, think about expensive experiments, and, most importantly, to consider carefully the design of each experiment.

ADMINISTRATION

The word administration fills young scientists with dread as they see endless mountains of paper and tedious hours of committee meetings. As you move up, administration is difficult to avoid, but it can be enormously valuable and informative, and sometimes even enjoyable.

For staff members in universities, research institutes or companies, only the incredibly talented, completely inept or very lucky can avoid jobs such as safety officer, seminar organiser or post-graduate tutor. Administration also includes activities such as serving on appointments or grants committees, editorial boards, committees of learned societies or advising industry or government. They all take time, but there are pay backs – an enormous amount can be learnt from each job and there are real opportunities to influence things. The important issues to consider with any such duties are attitude and efficiency. When a new job is undertaken it is likely to take a lot of time, particularly if it is important – though in fact every such job is important in itself and in the impression you will create. Comparisons will inevitably be made (and noted) between the young staff member who is sloppy in a job and the one who is efficient and effective. Such comparisons can have much greater impact than first imagined (e.g. in promotion). With a little experience, it is possible to dis-

tinguish those aspects of any administrative duty which are most important and take time and those which can be skipped over quickly.
Complaints about inefficient administration, bureaucratic processes and
time-wasting meetings are numerous, but do not fall into the trap of per-
petrating these failings. Many who take on administration for the first
time try to be over enthusiastic or to extend the importance of an administrative duty. Act efficiently and think of your time and that of others you
will influence. Chairmen of committees so often forget how they (as committee members) hated long and rambling meetings, volumes of paperwork and indecision. The best way to attract respect is to get the job done
well with the minimum of fuss, time and effort. The benefits of this to
your career cannot be underestimated.

LEAVING THE BENCH

Success in research, moving up the career ladder and taking on responsibilities, will almost inevitably mean moving away from the practical
aspects of research. To the committed researcher, this is the hardest part
of success because actually doing experiments and seeing the results is
what they most enjoy. A few senior scientists manage to avoid the usual
administrative duties, keep their lab quite small and still spend a significant amount of time doing experiments themselves or working directly
with those in their lab. But this is hard for scientists in most positions. In
universities, the demands of teaching add to the time spent writing grant
applications and papers, managing funds and supervising students and
post-docs. Then there is the need to attend and present at national and
international meetings. In the commercial sector the situation is likely to
be little different, with pressures of writing reports and filing patents, on
top of the normal supervision, presentations and administration.

The transition period is the most difficult. This is the time when a
scientist still considers themselves quite young – perhaps soon after
taking up an independent post with their own lab. All seems to be going
well when suddenly you realise that you have not conducted a full experiment for several months and have barely been in the lab over the last few
weeks. The unpleasant withdrawal symptoms do eventually decline, as
realism and acceptance sets in. Maintaining and protecting time for
doing experiments needs discipline and planning, setting aside specific
days or a block of time during a quiet period when everyone has to realise
that you are not to be disturbed. The other way is to do experiments 'off-
site' where you will not be disturbed. This can be done by arranging short
periods of working in a 'collaborative' lab or a more lengthy sabbatical

which is usually refreshing and invigorating, but not always easy to arrange around other commitments.

INTERNATIONAL RECOGNITION

The logical progression for a successful scientist is international recognition, when your name is known and respected by everyone in the field, your papers are read widely and you are flooded with invitations to give major lectures and keynote presentations. Of course the pressures are no less, they are just different. The grant applications still need to be written and funds obtained, the papers published and the students and post-docs supervised, in between international travel and numerous other duties. Hopefully by this stage you will have a well-structured lab with several senior post-docs and technicians, expert technical help and an organised approach to a busy schedule. You will have to learn to be selective in what you do and how to say no. If you do achieve such success, do not forget how you felt as a young, struggling scientist; how important it was when those you admired so much stopped to chat at your poster or praised you on a presentation. Success does not mean you should stop being nice to people.

FURTHER READING

On Being a Scientist (1996). Washington, DC: National Academy Press.

9

Funding research

Scientists are not wealthy of course, but the scale of their grants is usually so adjusted to make it possible to buy the equipment they need.

Research is expensive and funds normally need to be sought from external bodies. General infrastructure, things like buildings and their maintenance, libraries, computing facilities, administration, personnel, cleaners, porters and car parks, are usually funded by the institution. Increasingly, though, such costs have to be recovered from external sources, usually as indirect costs (or overheads) charged on grants. The direct costs of a research project pay the salaries of researchers (and sometimes part or all of the lab head), equipment and running costs (reagents, disposable items, computing costs, animals, cells, etc.). These will almost certainly have to be paid through grants sought by the principal investigator. Without such grants, very little research can be undertaken. The extent of funding required varies considerably from theoretical studies which may need just people, libraries and computing facilities, to astrophysics where large radio telescopes are extremely expensive and are almost always shared by a large consortium of scientists.

Securing external funding is also used as a measure of success in science. Significant income from peer-reviewed grants is an important part of a CV which greatly improves prospects of jobs and promotion. Money talks – even in science. Getting such grants is not so easy, particularly for the inexperienced. There is great competition for such funding, and award rates for some sources can be as low as 10%.

WHAT MAKES A GOOD GRANT APPLICATION?

The most important factor in determining the success of a grant application is the quality of the science. Good science normally gets funded, poor-quality science rarely does. But there is more to it than that. Even good (or excellent) scientists, conducting high-quality research, can struggle to get funds. Another factor is 'grantsmanship' – the ability to present the application in the best way at the right time to the right funding body.

The key features of good grants are the importance of the problem, timeliness, novelty, feasibility and presentation. Many applicants fail to explain 'the big picture', but instead get lost in the minute detail. Put the specific project into the broader context and say how it fits. Timeliness is important but tricky. There are undoubtedly 'trendy' or 'hot' areas in science at any time. These can be readily identified by browsing through a few issues of the major, interdisciplinary scientific journals. They are usually exciting and fast-moving areas, but are also intensely competitive. Some of the biggest and best labs in the world will be working in these areas, and will probably review your grant. This does not mean you cannot compete successfully in such areas, particularly if you have a track record of success in a good lab, and/or can develop your own niche, but you need to be aware of the intense competition. There is also a danger of being 'ahead of your time'. Proposals (especially from young scientists) which are too radical, or question accepted dogma, may be viewed unfavourably by established and sometimes conservative reviewers. There may be ways around this by acknowledging the risks and controversies and suggesting alternatives (see below), and some awarding bodies have schemes specifically for innovative and risky proposals.

NOVELTY AND FEASIBILITY

These two aspects of a grant can present a conflict. If every experiment is obvious and will undoubtedly succeed, the project is 'safe', but is probably not very new or exciting. On the other hand, novelty means excitement, but high risk. New approaches which may not work, experiments for which the outcome is not known, and difficulty in predicting the latter stages of the work make for an exciting project but one that is likely to cause concern and criticism by the reviews. A common and very useful piece of advice is to include 'something old and something new'. That is, a part of the project should be clearly feasible and achievable, with some evidence that preliminary experiments have been undertaken successfully, another part may be more risky. There is a general view that in the USA many grant proposals are for work that has been largely completed, whereas in other parts of the world, such as the UK, this is less likely to be the case. The truth of this is hard to determine, but probably has some basis. Particular care needs to be taken when *pivotal* experiments are risky. It is most unwise to present a proposal where the whole project depends on the first series of experiments for which the outcome is uncertain. The reviewers will quickly see that, if that first series fails, the project is doomed. The basis of the project needs to be sound, even if later parts are risky. Do not be afraid to say that an experiment is risky or that there are several possible outcomes, but do say what you will do as an alternative if it fails and how you will proceed in light of each possible outcome. *Contingency* is important (and an excellent section to include), i.e. explain what you will do if things do not go to plan. This shows that you have thought carefully about likely outcomes, problems and pitfalls and how you will deal with them.

FISHING EXPEDITIONS

This phrase comes up frequently at review panels, usually as a criticism of grants which are essentially observing phenomena, large screens or gathering data. Reviewers do not like fishing expeditions because they are not hypothesis based (i.e. they do not test a specific idea), they are rarely mechanistic, and they tend to *show* things rather than *explain* them. This has become something of an issue with the growing use of automated analyses of gene and protein expression, where the effect of some intervention will be tested on the response of a system and is likely to yield a vast amount of data (e.g. analysis of multiple gene expression). The main questions are what is the specific purpose of the experiment? What will you do with the data? How will you analyse it in a meaningful way (and this is a significant problem without considerable resource)? How will you then select from what may be hundreds or thousands of genes/proteins/responses which change (some of which may be of unknown function) those you will study next? This can of course be done in a number of ways, e.g. by selecting carefully the manipulation to reduce the likely number of responses. Then it is possible to select criteria for future studies, to carry out further manipulations and select those that change in each case (ideally including one interaction which could be predicted to cause a change in the opposite direction). Then you can select a handful to study further.

There are many other examples of 'descriptive' studies. Such studies are valuable or even essential, whether reviewers like them or not. But they can often be described in a way that makes them much more acceptable. For example, you can argue that these types of study are *hypothesis generating* rather than *hypothesis testing*. The key then is to say what you will go on to do once you have generated hypotheses. Descriptive studies can be rephrased – rather than saying, 'we will determine if A changes B...', it looks better (though in reality is the same) to say that, 'our hypothesis is that B mediates the effects of A on.... We will test this by...'. Wherever possible, do not include what might be seen as 'fishing expeditions' as a major part of a proposal.

WHO FUNDS WHAT?

Before sitting down to prepare a proposal, some background information is needed on the sources and types of funding available. In most countries, there are several options – government sources such as NIH or NSF in the USA, the Research Councils in the UK, etc. These tend to be the major funders with the biggest budgets and the widest portfolios of different types of funding. There are also many wealthy charities which fund research (the largest being the Wellcome Trust in the UK); international funding schemes, such as Human Frontiers Science Programme (HFSP); the European Union; some special foundations; and private industry. For most of these (industry being a possible exception – see below and Chapter 10) there are very clear guidelines on what they will fund, who is eligible and on how and when applications must be submitted. This information is extremely important. Do not just read the booklet or look at the web site. Telephone the funding body and speak to one of their programme officers. Read the information, make a set of questions then approach them directly. They are there to help you, and are usually knowledgeable, friendly and helpful. If possible, go and see them – there is nothing like face-to-face discussions to get things sorted out. Funding bodies often have special schemes and initiatives for young investigators and priority areas. Consider carefully the size of your proposal. There is no point in submitting for a major, expensive proposal to a small medical charity when their total annual budget is very limited. Check funding rates. This should not be a sole determining factor, but if they are below 10%, beware, though there may be funding bodies in one of your niche areas that do not receive many good proposals. Determine if an outline proposal is needed and check the deadlines carefully – there is rarely any flexibility on these. Find out what sort of things they will fund and what they will not.

For most young investigators, a modest, three year proposal is the best place to start, usually in the form of a project grant. Larger grants (e.g. five year programmes – see below) are difficult to obtain without a proven track record as an independent researcher. Fellowships are awarded to individuals for their salary and associated costs – again eligibility is important. There are likely to be limits on age (or more commonly now on your time in research) and sometimes on citizenship.

PLANNING AND PREPARATION

As with any form of writing, begin with a plan or outline. First, identify the question you are trying to answer, the problem you are trying to solve and the hypotheses you are going to test? Again remember – the *big* question first, then the *specific* questions. Next decide how you will do it. Flow diagrams may help, and often many versions will be necessary (ideally discussed with colleagues) before your ideas are really clear and you are ready to write. Sometimes it helps to write the summary (which is the most important part of the proposal) at an early stage, but it will almost certainly have to be rewritten later. Prioritise experiments and decide on a logical progression. Many funding bodies require a timetable of the work, with 'milestones' or 'check points' when specific aims should have been achieved or decisions need to be made. One series of experiments may be the most important, but there is no point in putting them first if they depend on the outcome of another series. Work through each experiment, thinking about the logistics – just how many samples, cultures or animals will you need, what control groups, analyses, etc.? This will help to determine if the project is feasible and workable.

Having established what you are going to do, decide how you are going to pitch it and sell it to the reviewers. Enthusiasm and clarity are essential, but do not overstate the case, and always be honest. There is no point in claiming that your research will lead to a cure for major diseases if this is clearly unrealistic. Instead state the *potential* relevance. Get feedback on your plan from experienced colleagues and leave plenty of time. Start well in advance of the deadline – at least a couple of months if you can.

REMEMBER WHO YOU ARE WRITING FOR

A failing of the less experienced is to write grant proposals for the handful of experts in their field. In reality, the panel of reviewers is likely to contain (at most) one or two who are such experts and in some cases none. Most will have a good general knowledge and will be able to assess the reports of expert reviewers. It is the panel who will make the final decision. The reviewers, to whom your proposal will be sent, will also appreciate a clear background and crisp statements rather than enormous detail. A good rule of thumb is to write for a faculty member in your general, but not specific, area, and include a few sections which illustrate that you do know and understand the field in depth. This is why it is important to get your proposal checked by a colleague who is not an expert. Avoid jargon and do not assume that the reviewers know that you know how to deal with problems – be explicit and specific. Avoid ambiguity or vagueness and try to give a value to everything. If the reviewers do not understand your proposal, they will assume that you have presented it badly or do not understand it yourself – not that it is their failing.

How you write a proposal may be influenced by the review panel. The membership of such panels is usually available. Get the information and consider it carefully. What is the background of the panel members, does the panel include real experts or major competitors in your field and can you identify the two members who are likely to be assigned your proposal to review in detail? These considerations should not dominate or radically revise what you write, but they will have an influence. If one of the panel members has a view which differs from your own or has conflicting data, address and discuss this rather than ducking the issue.

Members of most review panels will have a large number of proposals to read and assess. They probably dread the courier arriving with many kilogrammes of paper. But, even more than this, they dread turning to the proposal that they are assigned to review in detail, to see numerous pages of information in dense type, in a font that is barely readable (remember that most reviewers are likely to be middle-aged with less than perfect eye sight), with no clear plan, diagrams, headings or 'sign posts' to help them through the proposal. You must help the reviewer and the funding body to help you. Avoid any unnecessary detail or words, use sub-headings and summaries which act as 'sign posts' to lead the reader through the proposal.

As with interviews, opinions are formed quickly. The abstract or summary is likely to have a major impact on the reviewer and is therefore the most important part of the proposal. It is here that the reviewer will first consider whether your proposal is important, interesting, novel and timely; if the approaches look feasible and therefore likely to be funded. The title and abstract will also be used (perhaps with the references) by the project manager to decide which reviewers to send the proposal to, so think carefully about what you say.

AIMS, OBJECTIVES, HYPOTHESES

This section may come at the very beginning of the proposal or after the background section, depending on the format required. If it is at the beginning, start with a few lines of background to set the scene and lead into the objectives. It is useful to have an overall objective, i.e. 'the big picture', followed by your specific hypotheses. Then describe how they will be addressed. A sentence or two on likely outcomes may also be valuable, but do not just repeat what is in the summary. Avoid a long list of hypotheses and aims, three to five is usually the maximum that can be achieved, though these may have some sub-sections, particularly on a larger proposal. When this section is completed, keep it in a prominent position and refer to it as you are writing the rest of the proposal. A common failing of grant applications is that the experiments described do not address the aims and objectives. This problem develops as the grant is repeatedly modified during writing and rewriting, and a mismatch develops. The reviewer will be asked to comment on whether the proposal will answer the questions posed. All too often the answer is no.

BACKGROUND

Begin with simple, clear statements addressed at a general audience and state the problem 'upfront'. The whole of the background section should 'set the scene' for your project proposal, highlighting the key issues. It should not be an extensive review of the whole field; avoid jargon and limit abbreviations as much as possible (see Chapter 5).

Try to break the background down into sections with relevant headings. Summarise each section, in a few brief, highlighted sentences to help the reader. Figures included in the background can be informative, and may reduce and break up otherwise dense text. You will need to show what you have discovered, why it is new and important and include published and unpublished data and preliminary results. This shows your experience in relevant techniques as well as what you have discovered. It is essential to quote the work of others in the field – not least because some of them may review your proposal. The reviewers need to see that you recognise the work of others, address disagreements and discrepancies, and do not present a parochial review which could be viewed as naïve, or arrogant.

EXPERIMENTAL SECTION

The length, detail and presentation of this section varies significantly between funding bodies. In Europe a full project proposal (three year grant) would normally be described in a maximum of five pages, and a programme proposal (five year grant) usually in ten pages. In the USA, full proposals are very much (often three to five times) longer, and considerably more detail is required. The experimental section will therefore vary, but would normally take up a major proportion (e.g. two thirds) of the full application. The reviewers are assessing *what you are going to do,* not your ability to describe the field. So, while the background must set the scene and put your aims in context, the experimental section is the real 'guts' of the application.

It is quite difficult to keep this section readable and clear while including the necessary detail. It is helpful to keep the protracted (and often tedious) description of the methods separate, either at the beginning or (perhaps better) at the end. The extent of detail will depend on whether methods are established and non-controversial and whether the reviewer will be satisfied that *you* can actually use them. If all of this is readily established, a brief description of the methods to be used, perhaps with references and a statement of your experience or of any modification, is sufficient. A new method will need to be described in more detail, with justification to convince the reviewer that it is feasible and appropriate. Beware of brief statements, such as we will use 'transfected cell lines', or 'neutralising antibodies' or 'knock-out animals', without convincing the reviewer that you have them or can make and use them. If necessary, include collaborators who are experts, and provide a letter expressing their willingness to collaborate. But do not let your whole project depend on external collaborations, or the review panel may feel that they, rather than you, should get the grant. Be sure to describe exactly why collaborations are necessary, what they will do and provide strong evidence (letters) of their willingness to collaborate.

DESCRIBE YOUR EXPERIMENTS

The most important part of the proposal will describe the experiments to be done and the thinking behind them. These sections should map precisely on to the aims and objectives, so that the reviewer can see how each series of studies will address or answer the key questions/hypotheses. Short statements at the beginning and/or the end of each series of experiments to state their importance and outcome are helpful. Assign priority and order, i.e. state which experiments will be conducted first, which will run in parallel and which depend on each other.

At all costs, avoid vague statements such as, 'the effect of A will be tested on a number of possible mediators (e.g. B, C, D, E, F, etc.) in several cell lines'. It is better to select specific mediators, but defend your selection. If necessary, say that you cannot exclude the involvement of other mediators, which may be considered, but as lower priority (and name them). When appropriate, include preliminary data or evidence that an experiment or a technique will work. Say how you will analyse and interpret results. All too often an experiment may look appropriate and feasible, but closer inspection shows that it cannot yield a clear answer to the question, or the number of groups and parameters precludes valid statistical analysis. State the justification for group sizes (ideally based on power analysis of published or preliminary data). This will help to justify your costs and is particularly important for projects involving humans or animals.

The project must be focussed. A major failing of grant applications submitted by young scientists (and also some more experienced ones) is that they are over ambitious and simply not achievable. However, it is reasonable to have a section at the end which is a little more speculative and indicates where you hope to go in the future. This demonstrates that you have long-term as well as specific and defined goals.

WHAT TO ASK FOR

The purpose of all this grant application writing is to get money. The funding must usually be requested for the *specific project* described, and therefore must be justified on the basis of what you will do. However, it may be possible to request part-costs, e.g. a contribution towards the purchase of a piece of equipment or a technician's time. Check exactly what costs are eligible for centralised facilities, e.g. library, central computing animal, cell culture, sterilisation, sequencing facilities, etc. In the cases where you request part costs, show that you (or the institution) have, or will definitely get, the rest of the money. Whatever you request, it must be *justified* – you must show exactly why it is needed for your project. When deciding what to ask for, seek the advice of colleagues, look at their grants, and talk to the programme manager at the funding body to determine what is the normal range and what is acceptable. Most review panels have 'ball park' figures for the acceptable costs of projects. If you stick within this range and provide a good justification, you are likely to get what you ask for.

Staff are likely to be the major cost. The type (e.g. post-doc, technician) and seniority (grade) of the staff you request also depends on what they will do on the project. Bear in mind that you should state what *you* will do on the project. This may be simply supervision and direction, or you may plan (hope) to conduct some of the experiments yourself. Many applications require statements on the hours or proportion of your time spent on the project. For young investigators, this is likely to be quite high. But be careful – this can be a hostage to the future. A couple of years later, a reviewing panel can work out that more than 100% of your time will be spent on current projects. Describe not only what you and the staff requested will do, but show how they fit together and provide the skills that are needed. It helps to have named staff (with a good CV) included. Review panels often cut grants in order to fund a few more projects. One of the easiest ways to do this is to 'chop' one of the staff required. They are less likely to do this if the post is well justified and the person is named. Review panels are concerned about the careers of individuals, so give a brief description of named personnel and their institution.

Equipment will also have to be justified on the basis of the specific project. It is normally recognised that a new investigator will need more equipment than an established researcher, or that a project which takes a slightly different direction to ongoing work may require new equipment. Discuss why such equipment is not available in your department, or needs to be dedicated to your project. Similarly for recurrent expenditure and travel, reasonable costs (check the value with colleagues and programme managers) are likely to be accepted without serious scrutiny. The use of animals normally require very specific justification and discussions of why alternatives cannot be used, particularly in the UK. Try to explain any savings on the costs of research, e.g. reagents which have been donated free of charge, in-house assays which are cheaper than commercial alternatives or facilities/reagents which can be shared. A question the reviewers will have to answer is whether the project represents 'good value for money'. You need to convince them that it is. Good grants are rarely turned down because they are too expensive – they will just be cut, but there is a limit to costs, beyond which you will test the patience of reviewers.

PRESENTATION

Good presentation will not get poor science funded, but bad presentation has killed many potentially fundable proposals. Sloppy projects with mistakes or omissions imply that the applicant is likely to be sloppy in their science – even if this is not actually true. Poor presentation annoys reviewers, who have many applications to read, and means that your proposal may not get the review you feel it deserves. Leave time to read, check and get colleagues to review your application.

Issues about good presentation of a good grant are similar to those of a good paper (Chapter 5), and relate mainly to consideration of the reader. Be enthusiastic, but temper this with realism and self criticism. Be concise and brief, avoid lengthy sentences, unnecessary words and detail, overuse of abbreviations and long sections of text. Describe references as superscript numbers in the text; this saves space and avoids breaking up scientific discussion. It is not necessary to use the full page limit, and often better not to fill every available space on the page. *Never* exceed the page limit, use smaller font than indicated in the regulations or reduce margins. If you infringe these regulations and your grant application is not returned to you before it is reviewed (which it can be), it will certainly not please the reviewers.

Check and recheck the application. Look at what is missing, where are the pitfalls? Ensure that every relevant section is completed. Applications need detail in addition to the main sections, such as curriculum vitae, other grants held, reports on previous grants, collaborations, suggested reviewers, commercial exploitation, public understanding of science, lay summary, etc. Check that the correct number of copies, discs and any supporting information is sent on time (if necessary by courier). Then check that it was received.

Never knowingly submit a poor proposal. Resist the temptation to 'throw in a proposal' which you really think will not be funded. Such proposals may make an impression which can come back to haunt you in the future. The world of reviewers in your field is relatively small and they are likely to remember your earlier application.

ADDRESSING REVIEWERS' COMMENTS

Some funding bodies allow applicants to comment on the reports from external referees (*ad hoc* reviewers) before the application is considered by the panel, or may request resubmission in light of those reports and/or the panel's comments. A balanced and informative response is most valuable. You may believe that the reviewers were biased or failed to read or understand your proposal. But all too often they have raised valid criticisms or have failed to fully understand something because it was not explained clearly. Where more than one referee raises the same point, it is almost undoubtedly valid and must be addressed. Consider the reviewers comments carefully and try to see their point of view before responding. Responses should be brief, polite and to the point. This is an opportunity to answer specific points, not to write another proposal. Where possible use referees' comments against each other, e.g. referee A may say the project is ambitious and they do not like Section 2, while referee B says it is feasible, but is not so keen on Section 3. This can help you. Do not feel the need to answer every point or to provide excessive detail. Occasionally reviewers are unreasonable or even rude. Then it is acceptable to say that you feel they have been unfair and why, but not for you to be rude. Do not say you know who the reviewer is – you could be wrong. Reviewers nominated by the applicant are not necessarily supportive.

REJECTION

The majority of grant proposals submitted are not funded, for a variety of reasons. The funding body should provide some feedback, but this may be very brief and uninformative. If you telephone the funding body and get the bad news, do not berate or argue with the person who tells you. It is not their fault and you may need their help in the future. Even when all the reviewers' comments are transmitted to the applicant they may not have any major criticisms. Many applications are rejected not because there is anything seriously wrong with them, but just because they were not quite good enough against strong competition. Maybe they did not address a really important problem, were not considered as novel or such good value for money compared to others which scored higher and got funded. It can help to phone the programme manager at the funding body to ask for further feedback. They are likely to be helpful, and might say more over the phone than they would put in writing. Never contact members of the grant panel to ask for feedback or complain. Some funding bodies specifically exclude scientists from further applications if they make such contacts.

When a proposal is rejected there may be an opportunity for resubmission to the same body. This is common in the USA, but, in other countries, resubmission is rarely encouraged (e.g. most UK funding bodies). In fact resubmission has a low success rate, unless it is requested, usually with very specific feedback, which must be addressed in the new submission. If resubmission is not encouraged, it is usually better to consider applying to another funding body. In any case, a proposal should be resubmitted only after any criticisms have been addressed. It is quite likely to go to the same reviewers, who will probably not be too pleased to see it again.

BIG GRANTS

Major proposals include large programme grants involving many staff, extensive and ambitious experiments spanning a period of five years or more, funding for a centre or for several independent groups within a research unit. The same basic principles apply to big grants – excellent science, novelty, feasibility and clear presentation are essential. The potential difficulties with major proposals are to plan and describe a series of interlinked experiments which address major questions, exhibit depth and focus over a broader area, and are written in such a way that they cannot be chopped up by the committee into separate project grants. It is also difficult to predict experiments four or five years in the future. A clear plan has to be presented – though in reality it is likely that the situation will change significantly, unless it is a rather slow moving, and therefore potentially unexciting field. Sub-sections of a major grant proposal may be read separately by different reviewers, particularly if they involve different approaches, and it may be assessed by a large number of reviewers, each with expertise in specific sub-areas.

Major grants, centres and units are often renewable, generally at five yearly intervals with the renewal considered in year 3 or 4. In this case, the past work (on the ongoing programme) is likely to be reviewed and assessed as well as the future plans. For all proposals, the standing of the applicant and his/her ability to conduct the work will be considered. For programme grants, the applicant should be of a strong international standing with a highly productive record; the research will address a major problem, usually attacking this at several levels and in several ways.

FUNDING FROM THE COMMERCIAL SECTOR

Significant amounts of strategic, applied and even basic research in academia is funded by the commercial sector as studentships, fellowships, project, programme grants and major awards. The means of obtaining such funds are varied and rather different to the processes described above. Only rarely do companies select projects under open competition with external reviewers. More commonly collaboration will be developed between an academic team and their counterpart in industry. A dialogue then develops about the research and how it will be funded. Through an interactive process, the plan is formulated and the costs are agreed. On occasion, a company may simply ask for a proposal and costing, which is often much shorter than the equivalent application to other funding bodies. Subsequently there may be negotiation about experiments or costs.

However, universities almost always require significant *indirect* costs for industrially funded work in order to pay 'the real costs of the research'. Thus, indirect costs (overheads) may range from 50% to well over 100% of the direct costs. Sometimes they can be negotiated (usually between administrators in the company and the university). In other cases, the company or the university is fixed in what it will accept. Unfortunately these views may not match and in spite of extended discussions, the project may not go ahead. Even when the plan and costings are agreed, there may need to be complex discussions about the contract, but this would normally be undertaken by central administration rather than by the scientist. With industrial grants there may be additional issues of confidentiality, permission for publication, patents and intellectual property rights (see Chapter 10).

REVIEWING GRANTS

Once you have published a few papers and become known in your field it is likely that you will be sent grant applications to review. Speed, efficiency and confidentiality are probably even more important in reviewing grant applications than in refereeing papers (see Chapter 5). The review will have to be returned in time for the grants panel meeting. If you delay, the applicant may have to wait many months for the next meeting, by which time someone's salary might have run out and they will have lost their job. The funding body (to which you may submit your own proposal) will also not be too pleased. Grant proposals are highly confidential. They will contain ideas and plans for three to five years, and breaking confidentiality could get you barred from future funding from that body.

While the applicant will not know who the reviewers of his/her proposal are (though they can sometimes guess), the panel will know, and this may be the same panel that assesses your own grant applications. They will particularly value clear, concise and fair reviews and may remember how you responded as a reviewer when they later consider your own proposal. It is not usually necessary to write numerous pages in a grant review, but it is important to understand the guidelines from the funding body and address the questions they ask. These are likely to be the same questions as those discussed above which you should consider when writing a proposal.

Invitations to serve as a member on a grants panel (usually for a period of two to four years) need to be considered carefully. Such duties are very demanding and time consuming, but also usually enjoyable. They are an excellent way to learn about your field, and the best way to see how to write a good grant proposal.

FURTHER READING

Ogden, T.E. (1991). *Research Proposals : A Guide to Success.* New York: Raven Press.

10

Who owns science?

Tell everyone everything you know.

Who owns science seems like a simple question, but the answers can be complex and varied depending on the situation. As a student or post-doc you might believe that you and your boss (supervisor or lab head) jointly own the results, as a company employee it will seem obvious that the company has ownership (in most cases that is how they make their money) and as an independent scientist in academia the common belief is that the results are yours. In fact there are many stakeholders, particularly in academic research. The scientist who had the ideas, secured funding, supervised the work and inevitably analysed and disseminated (e.g. published) the results is of course a major stakeholder. But so too is the host institution which provides the facilities and support and often the salary of the scientist. The funding bodies (of which there may be several) may also have a claim on ownership. In most cases these issues do not matter. You, as the scientist and your team, will publish the results and use them as you see necessary for securing future funds, developing new hypotheses and plans, submitting for higher degrees or presenting at meetings. It does, however, matter when the findings have potential commercial value and can be exploited, when patents may be filed or when agreements are in place with companies.

CHANGING CULTURE

Traditionally, research within the commercial sector has been clearly aimed towards developing products or processes of value which will generate revenue (profit) for the company and the shareholders. In contrast, research in the academic sector has been called 'pure', i.e. curiosity driven with no obvious application or commercial value. In reality, much of academic research has applications (whether it is realised by the scientist at the time or not), and often has potential commercial value. Indeed, many scientists in academia now conduct research with the specific goal of understanding practical problems, such as human disease, and finding ways of treating them.

A significant change in thinking has been emerging over the last decade or so. Academic scientists are beginning to realise the financial value of their findings. They are working more closely with the commercial sector, and are now exploiting their findings to the financial benefit of their institution, their lab and in some cases to themselves. There is also growing pressure on the academic faculty to recognise, protect and exploit their findings. There are some notable examples of major discoveries by academic scientists (the development of monoclonal antibodies is commonly quoted) which were published without protection, and therefore could not be, or for other reasons were not exploited, with, in some cases, loss of huge potential income. The pressures to protect and exploit science come from all the stakeholders – the institution, department, the funding bodies and even the government, since these are all potential beneficiaries if the discoveries do actually make money.

It therefore seems obvious that every scientist should be aware of the potential application and commercial value of their work and first protect then exploit it optimally. Unfortunately, it is not always that simple. Protection and exploitation are not necessarily consistent with the aims of the academic scientist, which are to discuss and present data openly, publish as quickly as possible, supervise Ph.D. students and ensure they submit their theses on time and maintain the freedom to work in the areas of choice. Thus, there are potential conflicts to be resolved and the resolution is not always easy. An extreme view is that scientists in academia should focus on making discoveries which are rapidly disseminated and open to all, should work mostly on fundamental aspects of science without obvious relevance, applicability or commercial value, and those that wish to develop new products which generate income should leave academia for a career in industry. Of course such fundamental research is the very basis for application and commercial development, and it is often impossible to predict when a major breakthrough will come. The value of fundamental, curiosity-driven research should never be underestimated. It is often said that more funds for research should be diverted to studies which are relevant to improving the environment, human or animal health and welfare and the quality of life. This has been likened to the investor who tells his finance manager to invest in shares – but to choose only those which will increase in value. Science is the pursuit of knowledge – who knows what it will uncover? Who could have predicted that research to understand development of the nervous system of an obscure worm (*C. elegans*) would change our thinking about how cells live and die and would identify the key factors which regulate death (apoptosis) and survival in all living cells with wide-ranging applications to cancer and many degenerative diseases? Another argument is that every scientist (from any background) should be aware of the potential application of their work, has a duty to the community in which they work to recognise such applications and should attempt to exploit these in order to maximise the financial returns of their research, which is likely to have benefited from funding often from the public purse.

The reality is somewhere between these views. The value of basic, curiosity-driven research must be recognised and undoubtedly benefits from openness and dissemination of knowledge, but the scientist of today should also be aware of the application and commercial potential of his or her research.

OPENNESS AND SHARING

Leaving commercial considerations aside, a further issue for the scientist is how much to reveal openly about unpublished results and future plans and ideas. Scientists are (or should be) naturally enthusiastic about their research – wanting to share their findings with colleagues. There is some risk in this. Others may use your ideas and results in their own research. Sometimes those who do so are really unaware of what they have done (it is not always easy to identify where an idea originated or a project started). In other cases they know exactly what they are doing and feel that it is a fair playing-field to take whatever is on offer and run with it. When a major competing lab with extensive funding does this, you may lose out. Again this is a difficult balance. Openness and honesty is widely respected, and the losses are balanced by gains. Those who are sensitive and refuse to discuss what they are doing are often mistrusted and do not benefit from the openness of others. Scientists who discuss openly what they are doing and have discovered, share their reagents generously and welcome discussion, will sometimes lose out to an aggressive competitor, but will also benefit enormously from the respect of other scientists and a reciprocal sharing of information.

The decision over what to reveal or share depends very much on your position, that of your competitors and what is at stake. As a junior scientist the risks are greater – your competitors may be in a much better position to develop your ideas and findings and beat you to the major paper or patent. When a discovery has real commercial potential, revealing information could lose you the possibility of exploitation (see below). In general, openness and sharing is part of the culture of science, and examples of major disadvantages are fortunately rare. They should be put down to experience, but not necessarily change your basic views about open discussion. The availability and sharing of tools (e.g. recombinant proteins, antibodies, genetically modified animals) is now a major issue. Many journals demand that when you publish a finding, the reagents or information you include in that publication must be made available to the scientific community. Not everyone agrees with or adheres to this principle. Companies are likely to require an agreement that the products are released only subject to an agreement (see below) which can often restrict the use, ownership and publication of any work relating to the product. Even academic scientists are starting to use such agreements and require restrictions, though most scientists, particularly in academia, are happy to share what they have. Gene sequences now have to be made public (through databases) on publication, and reagents are normally made available to anyone who asks and explains what they want to do. But, if you are the one with the protein, antibody, clone etc. it is not always easy to adhere to these principles. The success of a current Ph.D. or post-doc project is likely to depend on further research using the reagents, so distributing them to a major competitor lab can present problems. The cost of providing and dispatching reagents can be significant. You can set up a system whereby the reagents are disseminated, subject to an agreement (e.g. for you to see the data before publication), to joint authorship, or to financial reimbursement for the cost of such reagents, or you can market them through a company. The options then depend to a large degree on the efforts (in time and money) put into generating the reagents, and the importance of them to you and your research group. In each case, it is wise to explain openly and honestly to those that request reagents the situation and why you are making any restrictions. For example, explain that you are very happy to provide what is requested, but that the reagents are critical to a current project and will therefore be delayed, they are costly to produce so you will require some reimbursement or are subject to a secondary agreement which precludes dissemination. Do not just ignore requests or you will get a bad name. Most scientists are reasonable and will understand. However, it is not really justified (or beneficial to you) to claim authorship on every paper which uses an antibody that you developed.

THE VALUE OF DISCOVERIES

Scientists outside the commercial sector tend to be ill-informed about the value of their findings and how to exploit them, and are bewildered by the jargon involved. Such issues are usually handled by experts within your institution and/or the funding bodies, but such experts cannot act effectively without informed input from the scientist. It is therefore important for you to be aware and informed about issues such as confidentiality, intellectual property, exploitation, patents, technology transfer, licensing and assignment, venture capital and other aspects of the seemingly bewildering area of commercialism. Within a company these areas are dealt with efficiently and effectively by informed exchange between the scientist and the relevant expert. In the academic environment this is not always the case. Knowledge and understanding of the pros and cons and basic principles of exploitation do not mean that the academic scientist has to become expert in the details or devotes great time and effort. Relying on experts is fine, but the interface is not always easy, and successful interchange is dependent on both parties having some knowledge of the basic principles.

INTELLECTUAL PROPERTY

Scientific ideas and discoveries have intellectual value just as property in the form of materials or processes has value. Products such as chemical compounds, biological materials, new equipment and computer programmes have obvious value as materials. Products of the mind are termed *intellectual property* (IP), and can include names, inventions, 'know how' (i.e. expertise), methods and ideas. All have potential value. The right to use this property is known as intellectual property right (IPR).

The value of IP depends on several factors, such as novelty, applicability (e.g. is it a potential cure for a major disease) and protection. Speaking or writing in the public domain (known as disclosure) invalidates most IP for exploitation (with some exceptions in some countries). In academic science, ownership is defined by publication, after which the community should recognise the author as the discoverer of the idea and acknowledge them as such. However this often relies on the honesty and integrity of other scientists who sometimes choose to ignore earlier publications in favour of their own work, or may be ignorant of the first publication, particularly if it is not in a major journal. In commercial terms, the situation is somewhat clearer because of legislation. Most countries have laws on ownership (though they may be subject to varied interpretations).

The 'owner' may be (as in the USA) the first to discover or, as in most countries, the 'first to file' their discovery. The commercially accepted means of declaring and securing ownership is through the patent system.

PATENTS

A patent is a way of protecting your ideas and discoveries. It is not in itself a means of exploitation, but can prevent others from using the discoveries, and paves the way for you to benefit. Patents may cover products of the mind, inventions and methods, as well as new materials and products, in an agreement between the scientist and the government of the country in which it is filed. The value of a patent is only as good as the potential value and the opportunities for exploitation.

Patents originated over 500 years ago as a means for protecting ideas and discoveries, and their regulation and use is now accepted worldwide. The basic principles of a patent are very similar in different countries though the regulations vary slightly, so patents must be filed in each area of the world in order to obtain international protection. However, according to the Patent Corporation Treaty (PCT) a patent filed in one country may establish the priority date (see below) worldwide. A patent must be prepared according to specific regulations and is a commercial tool which establishes a monopoly on a discovery for a specified period of time, usually twenty years from the date of filing. If granted, the patent prevents others from using or exploiting ideas in the patent. It is also a unique source of information and technical detail which can be viewed and interrogated by others. Thus, a patent can protect ideas and promote research and development. It can also be traded, i.e. sold or assigned to others for commercial (or other) gain.

The requirements for filing a patent are common to most countries. They require that discoveries are novel, not obvious, and usable. Novelty means not only that others have not discovered or suggested what you have found, but also that the information has not been publicly described (though there is an exception to this in the USA). Not obvious means that those 'skilled in the art' (i.e. the experts in the field) would be unlikely to have come to the same conclusion based on the information available in the public domain. Usable means that it is necessary to show how the discovery can be used for practical and commercial benefit. The latter may be difficult with a new discovery. It is necessary to show (or even speculate) how the potential benefit (e.g. how it may be used to diagnose or treat a disease) and how 'one skilled in the art' could reduce the discovery to practice (effectively use). This may mean suggesting how the treatment might be delivered to a patient and in what doses. In reality this is likely to be very broad and speculative since detailed information will not normally be available at the time of filing.

THE INVENTION PROCESS

The process of an invention has certain definitions which are important in patent law. First there is the conception – who had the idea and when. Then there is 'reduction to practice' – doing the experiments which show that it works, together with checking that it really is new. The latter will mean rigorous checking, not only of the published literature, but also of patents filed and granted. Finally, the patent will be written and submitted, probably first in your own country and later in the major countries (e.g. USA, Canada, Japan and Europe).

All of this, and particularly writing the patent and dealing with any objections (which may be made by the patent examiner and will require written responses and/or amendments to the patent) needs expert advice. Within companies, the patent will almost certainly be handled by a group of experts who devote all their time to such issues. Most academic institutions now have similar departments dealing with all aspects of 'technology transfer' and intellectual property. If the academic institution does not have the expertise or finances to deal with patents, the body that funded the work almost certainly will have and will be only too willing to help.

Because of the complex legal aspects, jargon and specific requirements of patents, engaging such experts is essential for anyone who does not have extensive experience. But it is still important that the scientist understands the basic principles of the process and their implications. It is only through effective dialogue that success will be achieved. Some patent agents will have no scientific background (but are usually very good at interpreting and rephrasing science) and depend on the information they are given from the scientist. Never hold anything back in these discussions, e.g. data you may have disclosed in an open forum, other funders, collaborators or discussions with industry. The patent agent needs to know everything – even if you inadvertently disclosed your potentially valuable invention at a meeting.

ESTABLISHING PRIORITY

This really means proving that you made the discovery first and establishing the date. This is extremely important, particularly in the USA where patents are granted on the basis of 'first to invent' rather than 'first to file a patent' as in most of the rest of the world. Thus you may claim priority over another patent which is already filed, if you have written and verified evidence that you made the discovery at an earlier date. In order to establish priority you must have excellent records.

KEEPING RECORDS

The best records of scientific discovery are the standard lab book. The importance of these records was discussed earlier (see Chapter 3), but for protecting ownership and filing patents, the requirements are particularly rigorous. Lab books must be bound, with no pages removed, written in indelible ink with all deletions and modifications made clearly and visibly so the correction can be seen. Cross through any blank spaces and never use 'liquid paper' to make corrections. Number and date every page, sign it and get it witnessed by someone not directly involved in the project, preferably on the same date. Lab books need to be quite detailed. They should include ideas and objectives, descriptions of methods (unless these are well established), all results (including original data) and timeliness of the experiments. Keep every record – if these are separate, refer to them in the lab book and date and cross refer to the lab book on the separate records. Never delete electronic information or throw any records away.

CONFIDENTIALITY AND DISCLOSURE

Establishing novelty of a discovery for a patent means that you should not have discussed this information publicly, except in the USA where a patent can be filed up to one year after public disclosure. Publication in the scientific literature, or revealing results at major public meetings obviously act as disclosures, but other instances are less obvious. Data presented on web sites or at small group discussions can represent disclosure and even submission of papers or grant applications, letters or emails which are not marked confidential may be used to question priority.

If the research is of commercial interest you may want to discuss it with others in academia or industry, prior to filing a patent. This can be done without invalidating a future patent by obtaining a confidentiality disclosure agreement (CDA) which will be signed by the group you are talking to (most academic institutions can deal with this), and prevents them from releasing or using anything you tell them. This seems rather formal to academic scientists, but it is normally required by companies to protect their own findings, so it is not unreasonable that the academic community should also protect theirs.

WRITING THE PATENT APPLICATION

This will almost always be done by an expert – normally the patent agent. It can be a rather long and boring process which must adhere to the requirements of patent law. Basically the patent (which is a legal document) has several sections and requirements. The *specification* is the main substance – it *describes* the invention (discovery). This will require some detail. There will then be a set of claims which *define* the innovation, several claims may be independent or closely related. There will probably be a brief description of how the discovery was made (examples of experiments) often with figures or diagrams and results, and a discussion on how it can be used. This latter point may be very broad and somewhat vague if details are not yet available. The patent must have sufficient detail so that someone with the relevant experience could make and/or use the innovation. Thus, the patent not only establishes priority of an innovation it is also an excellent source of information which may not be present in a scientific publication (and indeed may never be published in the scientific literature). Approximately 80% of all technological developments are published only as patents and most companies regularly search patents for new discoveries.

INVENTORS AND OWNERSHIP

A patent will almost always be owned by your employing institution or company, unless you can demonstrate that the work has been undertaken in your own free time without use of any of your employer's facilities. The employer will pay the costs of the patent (which can be considerable if it is maintained for a number of years), deal with all aspects of filing and approval and will cover any insurance. The inventor(s) will be the person(s) who made the discovery. Deciding who should be an inventor is not always easy and not necessarily the same as authors on a paper. While many people may have contributed to a piece of work, to qualify as an inventor they must have been part of the *inventive step*, i.e. have been part of the intellectual input rather than they simply conducted the experiments or provided technical skills. If a patent generates income (see below) this may benefit the inventors. Academic institutions usually have fixed arrangements for patent revenue (usually calculated after the costs of the patent have been deducted), so that a portion of the income may be retained by the funding body and/or the university, a portion distributed to the inventor's department, some to his or her lab and sometimes a defined fraction to the individual inventors themselves. Patent revenue may also have to be shared between institutions in the case of co-inventors.

WHAT HAPPENS TO A PATENT?

Once a patent is filed, things tend to go quiet for quite a long time. Then it may be granted (approved), or more likely the patent examiner may come back with objections ranging from trivial changes in wording to major concerns, requesting extra detail and/or experiments. These processes can become quite protracted and eat into the life time (twenty years) of the patent. Hopefully the patent will eventually be granted, but this is really just the beginning. Few academic institutions have the facilities and resources to develop an invention through to market. For example, in the case of developing a potential new drug, vast resource and many years of toxicology studies and clinical trials are required. Even if all these are successful, the drug still has to be licensed by regulatory bodies, produced in large quantities of sufficient quality for clinical use, marketed and distributed.

More commonly the patent is *assigned* to another party (usually a company), i.e. ownership is transferred, or *licenced*, where ownership is retained but the second party is granted a licence to use the invention. In each case, income is usually generated for the holder of the patent. Negotiations over such transfers can be difficult and protracted as both sides barter for the best deal. Numerous options exist for payment, including a single, one-off sum, staged payments depending on success at defined milestones in the development of the invention, or royalties (usually between 1% and 10%) from the eventual income of the invention. The relative benefits of these options depend on the likely chances of success, the investment required for exploitation and the potential income to be generated.

WORKING WITH COMPANIES

The mutual distrust which was common between academia and industry in the past is declining significantly as both sides realise the benefits of collaboration and interaction. The commercial sector commonly provides grants for research in academia (see Chapter 9), which may be proposed by either side, then agreed by discussion between the two parties and the host institution. In addition to direct funds (and usually significant indirect costs for the institution), and exchange of skills, facilities and reagents, such interactions can provide a lever for additional funds. For example, many countries or groups of countries (e.g. European Union) have funding schemes which require ongoing or planned industrial collaboration, where costs are shared, or funds are available for research or studentships on the basis of industrial income. Contract research is usually defined much more precisely by the company, which will contract a scientist (and his or her lab) to undertake a specific piece of work, often under strict confidentiality with a limited possibility of publishing, or sometimes not even knowing what the experiment is about. In this case, funding levels are usually much higher because the only benefit to the academic is significant income.

Almost all interactions with industry will require a formal contract, the nature of which will depend on the type of interaction. The contract will lay down what is to be done (often the details of the research proposal or contract will be included in an appendix), by whom and when. It will have statements on publication, which you will need to read carefully. The company will almost always want to see and approve draft publications before they are submitted (so they can decide whether to patent a discovery or delay the disclosure of a potentially beneficial finding), but it is the time required for this approval which is important and can range from a few weeks to several years. Approval times of four to twelve weeks are normally acceptable and companies often act more quickly than that.

Ownership (IP) of the results is likely to form a major part of the contract. Normally if the company is paying and providing reagents, they will want the rights to use the results as they see fit. Contracts which are better for the academic institution and the scientist may be negotiated to include shared IP, and/or payments to the academic and his/her institution if the findings yield income. There can be fine details within these claims which need careful scrutiny and consideration. For example, check clauses on ownership of 'background IP' (that is the knowledge you had or discoveries you made before the contract was established), which should always be protected. Companies are likely to require confidentiality on anything they tell you, but the reverse may not be in the contract, so that in theory they could use whatever you tell them even when information is revealed inadvertently. Any reasonable administrator handling such contracts should be aware of these pitfalls and negotiate better terms. In the majority of cases, companies will not use such clauses to damage scientists, but it is better to be safe than sorry.

Supply of reagents free of charge from companies or academics usually requires agreement to a Materials Transfer Agreement (MTA). The MTA will probably cover what the compound can be used for, who owns the results, statements on publication, together with restrictions on passing the reagents to a third party. All too often, academics forget about the MTAs they have signed, sometimes many years before, and inadvertently breach what is a formal legal agreement. Difficulties can also arise when materials from several companies are used together in the same experiment or by someone funded by another company. These potential conflicts need to be considered very carefully. If doubts or concerns arise, consult expert advice, if possible before the experiments are begun.

CONSULTANCIES

Academics are frequently asked to act as consultants for industry in order to share their expertise and know how. Consultancy agreements (which again will probably involve a formal contract and/or confidentiality agreement) can cover anything from a short visit to a company to present a seminar and/or discuss a specific project or piece of work, to an ongoing and annually renewed consultancy agreement which may require you to review data, ideas and research directions, discuss new compounds, current markets, competitors etc. The nature of the contracts and size of financial reimbursements for consultancies vary depending on the activity, the size of the company and the seniority and value of the scientist.

Consultancies can be held independently by academic scientists, but permission is almost always required from your employer. If possible, it is better for the consultancy to be arranged through your employer (even if this means that the money is paid into your research account, rather than to you personally), because they will then check any agreements and cover insurance in the event that you get into difficulties or are sued by the company. It is only fair (and much easier in the long run) if you declare any ongoing industrial collaboration to any other company that approaches you (though of course the details of that collaboration will be confidential). This promotes openness and helps to avoid problems or conflicts in the future.

MAKING MONEY

Few scientists enter research in academia believing that they will become rich. However, some are now making significant sums of money, either from patenting and exploiting their results or from forming their own companies. All of these activities take time and effort, so they need to be considered carefully. Academic institutions usually encourage exploitation, but there may come a point when the time spent on such activities cannot be justified for a full-time academic scientist. This normally arises when a company is formed and the efforts needed to make this a success require full-time effort, which means making the difficult decision of whether to leave a secure (if rather poorly paid) position in academia to enter the world of business.

Setting up your own company can be extremely exciting and rewarding, but it requires considerable expertise as well as hard work and a certain amount of luck. You will need all the advice you can get, preferably from those who have been successful in the past, and a clear view of your goals. Starting small is of course easier, but for any company that is going to make money you will need to establish the value of the company, i.e. what is it based on? This may be simply your expertise and know how as a consultant, on research services, reagents or other intellectual property (generally in the form of patents). You need a business plan, financial and scientific advisors, a name for the company (which can be quite important), formal registration, and, most importantly, you will need money – start-up funds. Most small businesses fail because of under investment – the money runs out too quickly, long before any income is generated.

Modest start-up funds may be provided by your institution, funding body or even government sources, from early assignment or licensing of IP, from loans (but the repayments can be steep), but most commonly from investors who provide money in return for equity (a stake in your company and a share of potential profits). Investors – often known as 'business angels' or venture capitalists – are not charitable. They are usually shrewd businessmen or women who want their investment to give good returns. You will have to 'sell' them your ideas then negotiate a deal which will include realistic estimates of likely income and pay back and 'exits' (i.e. when they can get out and what with).

Unlike normal contracts with companies, or filing a patent, which can be undertaken largely by local staff with experience in these matters, raising capital for your company means *you* spending time and effort. Investors want to see the lead people (the scientists) who have the ideas. This will encroach more and more on your academic duties, on the time you have for research and for your lab, and can turn out to be a full-time job. The climate in the USA is generally more favourable for small start-up companies, particularly in the biotechnology area. Other parts of the world, such as Europe, have lagged somewhat behind. There are exciting stories of scientists who have made their millions, but these are rather few compared to those who make no money. But in many cases the latter group benefited enormously from the experience and, provided they did not mortgage their house, probably did not lose out.

FURTHER READING

Sullivan, N.F. (1995). *Technology Transfer: Making the Most of Your Intellectual Property.* Cambridge: Cambridge University Press.

Bryant, J.L. (1999). *Protecting Your Ideas: the Inventor's Guide to Patents.* New York: Academic Press.

Ducor, P. (2000). Co-authorship and co-inventorship. *Science* **289**, 873–5.

Stern, J.E. and Elliott, D. (1997). *The Ethics of Scientific Research.* London: University Press of New England.

On Being a Scientist (1996). Washington, DC: National Academy Press.

11

Science and the public

The ideas of the educated lay public on the nature of scientific enquiry and the intellectual character of those who carry it out are in a state of dignified, yet utter, confusion.

Scientists sometimes feel a little aggrieved that most ordinary folk are so little interested and impressed by their calling.

Science affects every aspect of life, at least in the Western world. Most of this is taken for granted. Some aspects, such as new medicines for people and their animals, better transport systems and faster computers, are valued enormously by the 'general public' (i.e. those who do not participate directly in scientific activities). Other facets can be disliked, distrusted and even feared, such as genetically modified foods, cloning, or the use of animals in research.

As scientists, we are members of society and have a responsibility to that society. This includes not only acting in an ethical and responsible manner, but also disseminating and explaining what we do and discover, the implications and applications of our research and the potential benefits, and being honest and open about potential disadvantages or failures.

THE CHANGING SCENE

The responsibilities of scientists to society at large have changed significantly in recent years. Just a decade or so ago, most of the scientific community would assume it perfectly acceptable to work on whatever they chose (as long as they could obtain sufficient funds), without concerns about the potential impact of their discoveries or about explaining their research to non-scientists. Hence it was considered justified to remain within the 'ivory towers' of academia, simply discovering, understanding and inventing, whilst believing that anything outside this was the responsibility of others – of policy makers, governments and teachers. Indeed some still adhere to this view. But in the twenty-first century things are very different and even the most reluctant scientists are being dragged (occasionally kicking and screaming) into the public arena.

There are several reasons for this change in culture. The public is becoming more aware, more knowledgeable and often more concerned about the impact of science and technology on their lives. The recent controversies surrounding genetically modified foods provides a good example. A few scary headlines (e.g. 'Frankenstein foods') and articles in the tabloid press lead quickly to widespread public concern about such foods. Recent publicity in the UK was based largely on 'scientific experiments' conducted by one researcher in Scotland. Arpad Pusztai's claims that rats fed genetically modified potatoes suffered damage to their guts was subsequently found (through extensive review) to have no scientific basis. Yet the debate continued to run. Neither the commercial organisations involved (whether crop producers or retailers) nor national governments succeeded in reversing the wave of public feeling which had developed. In this case, as in many others, scientists cannot turn their backs, but have to become involved in the discussions, and most importantly in explaining the scientific basis for new discoveries and their implications. Entering the public debate on such scientific issues needs to be embraced with caution and thought.

Governments have been quick to recognise the importance of public understanding of science and many funding bodies now require evidence that grantholders participate in some aspects of public understanding of science. There are even suggestions that a significant proportion of such research funds (e.g. 5%) must be dedicated to educating the public. After all, it is the public purse which provides research funds either through taxation, donation or consumer purchases, so it is not unreasonable that the scientists who use such funds should make some return.

PROBLEMS FOR THE SCIENTIST

Scientists now must face up to their expanding role within society, but a great deal is expected of them – sometimes unfairly. The growing embracement of public understanding of science has brought much criticism of scientists; claims that they are disinterested in discussing what they do or in explaining their research, that they refuse to appear in the media and that when they do, they are tongue-tied, boring and unable to give a straight answer.

Such criticisms are unfair. Scientists are trained and employed to do research, not to appear on TV or talk to school children. We are already very busy and often have difficulty communicating with our scientific peers, let alone to an audience who may have had no formal scientific education after leaving school. Some aspects of science (e.g. research on animals) can bring unwelcome attention and actions (see below). But things are changing. Many institutions now provide training to scientists in public presentations or dealing with the media, and such activities are beginning to be recognised and rewarded. Those who do find some time in their busy schedule to communicate with non-scientists usually find it extremely rewarding and are surprised to discover how much their efforts are appreciated by the public.

THE PUBLIC VIEW OF SCIENCE

To non-scientists, even those with a good education and an inquisitive mind, science seems to be something of a mystery, perpetuated by the ridiculous amount of jargon we all use. Scientists have not generally fared well in the media. Most films portray the scientist as either evil and power-mad or absent-minded and nutty. Children asked to draw a scientist often sketch an elderly, always male, rather eccentric character, usually with fluffy hair, glasses and leaking pens. It is therefore particularly important that younger scientists and women participate in presenting their work. In spite of these views on scientists (which are not always wildly inaccurate) and the apparent mistrust of science by the public, being open about science has many potential benefits. Recent surveys suggest that the public *do* trust and respect scientists, though opinions vary somewhat between countries, age groups and socio-economic backgrounds. Clearly there is a long way to go before the scientist acquires the public respect of clinicians or vets.

There are still relatively few science programmes on TV or radio. 'Scientific heroes' in the media are rare and how often do we see a popular soap opera based around science? These factors may contribute to the fact that children in many countries are not opting for further education or careers in science – particularly the physical sciences.

GETTING INVOLVED

If you are interested in getting involved in public understanding of science, it is wise to get some training first or at least watch others who do this successfully. Holding the attention of a group of school children or people off the street is not quite the same as speaking to a scientific audience (and many scientists fail dismally even with the latter).

Start with something quite easy such as writing a short article about what you do for a lay audience and ask non-scientist friends and family to give you their views. Your institution or national funding bodies are likely to run courses on scientific writing or presentations to the public and most countries have funding for such activities (e.g. the British Association in the UK). Many universities have links with local schools and are always looking for speakers – particularly if they are young and enthusiastic. They will usually offer training and advice. It is worthwhile going along to hear someone with experience address a group of school children.

PRESENTING TO NON-SCIENTISTS

The basic skills and rules here are not so different to those which apply to any form of public speaking. First know your audience – what age group, what background, how many will be there, will they have had any preparation? Then plan carefully and, as with scientific talks (but even more so), *less is best.* Keep it short and to the point. Non-scientists and even quite young children have a remarkable ability to follow quite complicated science provided you avoid any jargon, make your presentation colourful and interesting and keep to a few clear messages.

We are excited about what we do. That enthusiasm needs to come across in your presentations. After all most people like a good detective story and research is very much like detective work. One of the most important things to remember is to *tell a story*. Do not just give your audience facts – set the scene. What is the problem you (or others) have been trying to crack? Why is it important and different, and what did you do? Take them through the discovery and excitement, if possible telling them some of the unexpected things, something of the competition. Explain how scientific discoveries sometimes come from unexpected sources, about the race to make a new discovery with a scientific team in another country.

Most children above the age of about fourteen can follow what is essentially a simple research seminar that you would give to your scientific colleagues. You need to illustrate your talk – perhaps with some cartoons or an amusing story, limit the jargon and simplify the results. But basically if you have a scientific story to tell and can tell it in an interesting way, they will follow and appreciate it.

Children under the age of fourteen are in some ways more difficult, but can be the most appreciative audiences. They are less inhibited than older children but also have a much shorter attention span. For them you will probably need to show rather than just tell them things. Experiments and demonstrations always go down well, particularly if they are colourful, involve simple experiments on themselves, and if feasible an explosion or two! But do beware of health and safety. They are particularly delighted when something does not go to plan. This also gives you the opportunity to explain that science is not predictable! The most useful advice I have been given about communicating with non-scientists is to try to show rather than tell, to unravel a story so they want to know what happens next and to explain what science is really like. Sometimes the answers are difficult to find, sometimes they are not black and white, scientists do not always agree and the unexpected often happens.

Setting up experiments and demonstrations is great fun – for you and for the audience. But it is also very time consuming and expensive. Many funding bodies will now provide financial support for such activities, and time spent in building equipment, setting up experiments or animating presentations is usually worthwhile, and they can be used many times over. A valuable way of interacting with the public is for you (perhaps with a few colleagues) or your students to set up a stand in a busy shopping centre. Use catchy titles and large, colour posters, short simple statements and be ready to answer tricky questions. It helps to have some further reading (again brief and simple) for people to take away – this may be on some aspects of your own research, on a major topic (e.g. what is the human genome and why should I care?), or on a controversial topic such as genetically modified foods. Be prepared for tough questioning on some areas.

TRICKY AREAS

You may feel brave enough to tackle some of the more sensitive issues head on. Here some professional training and information packs really help. For example, many scientists go to schools with the specific purpose of explaining why we need to use animals in biomedical research. This is particularly important since they are likely to have many visits from those opposed to such activities.

When you do address sensitive areas, whether it is animals in research, genetically modified organisms, the use of foetal tissue, cloning or xenotransplantation, rather than simply presenting the issues try to get your audience to think and discuss them. A simple question such as do you think we should use animals in research will bring a range of answers. Most will probably say either no or only for developing new treatments for diseases. Get them to think about how medicines (for their pets as well as humans) are discovered. They will almost certainly be against the use of animals for cosmetic testing (which no longer takes place in the UK anyway), but ask them if they think if something like sun-screens are cosmetics. Do they need to go into the sun? But what about people with skin diseases who have to use sun screens? Soon they will realise that things are not quite as simple or as black-and-white as first believed.

Wherever possible use imagery and analogy. Often a complex problem can be explained in terms of everyday life events with which everyone is familiar. This is particularly useful for tricky concepts, such as risk, chance and probability. For example, people do not understand why scientists so often seem to get things wrong. It is important to explain to them that few things are certain. Ask anyone if it will snow in June in England and the answer will be no or probably not – but it can do and it has done. Relate science to people. Here you may be able to talk about our own work or that of colleagues. Paint a picture of who scientists are and what they are like. Historical stories also help, particularly when the story can be illustrated or embellished. Children find it much more interesting to hear how advances in human anatomy and physiology were made by cutting up dead bodies – sometimes stolen from graves – than to see a complicated diagram.

Often the best way of dealing with sensitive issues is to put them into context. So if you work in a medically related area it should be relatively easy to explain how we can use patients, tissue from post mortems and cell lines to try to discover the cause of a disease and develop a new treatment. But if you make your audience realise the limitations of such approaches and why animals are, unfortunately, still needed for some aspects of the research, they are much more likely to appreciate and accept their use. Indeed we should probably avoid the term public *understanding* of science. We cannot expect anyone other than an expert in the field to fully understand the complexities and details of current research. What we should strive for is public *appreciation.* Appreciation of why and how research is done, what it can and cannot discover or reveal, what the problems and potential implications are and how we can deal with them.

Presentations to the public or school children should not be too long (usually thirty minutes is long enough) unless you have experiments and demonstrations to keep the audience entertained. At the end they may have questions for you – often these are far more numerous, varied and tricky than after any scientific talk, and you may still find a queue of people wanting to talk to you even after lengthy questions. Teenagers are notoriously shy, so, if there are no questions from the audience, invite them to come up individually at the end of the talk in order to save their embarrassment.

DEALING WITH THE PRESS

Newspapers carry a surprising number of articles about science, and probably more so now than ever before. But to get into the national press you need to have a real story. The best way to get your research into the press is through a press release. This is usually a short statement (about one page maximum) describing your discovery in a short, punchy style. Academic and commercial institutions and funding bodies usually have press officers who are expert in writing press releases and getting them noticed. The press release has to say what, who, where and why – in a very short space. They usually include just one idea or finding, stating why it is important and if possible including some personal angle. More than any other form of writing, press statements must be brief – as a general rule subject, verb, object and little else, e.g. 'scientists in USA discover possible treatment for stroke'. Then a little detail to follow. Science correspondents on major newspapers often receive hundreds of press releases – most will go in the bin.

The press release is usually distributed via a press agency and/or posted on a news web site. It must include details of a contact person – and if this is you, you will need to be available for follow up interviews. If you have no experience of this it may be better to give the name of the press officer as a first contact. The distribution, follow up and timing of a press release are all important in getting attention. Early in the week is usually the best time to release because there may be not so much news from the weekend. However, you cannot plan for a major disaster or government announcement which will tend to push out anything other than a major scientific breakthrough.

If the story is followed up, journalists may call you for further information. Be very careful when talking to them. It is perfectly reasonable for them to quote anything you say, some of which you may regret later. Think about every question, even when you think the interview is over. It is highly unlikely that you will be able to check the article (though some science journalists do allow this), but you can ask to check any specific quotes of what you have said. It is best to establish this at the beginning of the interview. If you do see the draft article you can correct factual errors or misspellings and can reasonably expect that any misquotes will be changed, though this does not always happen. It is unlikely that the journalist will change something that you said, but did not mean to. They will probably have taped the conversation and can check exactly what you said. It can be worthwhile for you also to keep a tape of what you said.

Do not be too surprised if the finished article never appears in press. Science correspondents jostle for space just like any other journalists, and the decision about what goes in or not is down to their editor. You may also be surprised at how the story is presented, usually with a catchy headline which you may feel is inappropriate. Some controversial angle may be added to your story which you do not welcome. You are trying to get your findings noticed, but the journalist needs to get readers. These two goals are not always compatible.

Before making any contact with the press, TV or radio, check and get clearance from your institution. This may be a formal requirement of employment and can be of great importance in areas of sensitivity.

TV AND RADIO

Scientists are quite often asked to appear on TV or radio documentaries about science, usually to describe or comment on new discoveries. Such programmes are often recorded well in advance, involve sometimes extended discussions with the production team and agreement about the content and context of your contribution. Rather more difficult is the TV or radio interview, especially if it is about a controversial subject, and of course even more so if it is live. Avoid these unless you have training and practice, or are extremely brave. Find out as much as you can about the programme in advance, about other guests (you may not be told that someone will be invited to give an opposing view to yours). Make sure you know all about the topic of the programme, the length of your interview, the content of other parts (e.g. will there be film shown, etc.), the likely audience, and if possible ascertain what questions will be asked in advance. You can even request a contract which states exactly what you will be asked, but this will not always be granted. Check if you will have any editorial input on a recorded programme and of course ask what the fee will be. Scientists do not usually get paid much for TV or radio unless they become well-known presenters or have their own series, but you should get some payment and all expenses covered. When you are on television it is important to speak slowly, do not fidget and never get aggressive or argumentative, however provocative the questions may be. Try to meet the interviewer well in advance and make friends with them. Find out their views and angle and what they aim to achieve. If possible check them out with colleagues.

Presenting science to non-scientists requires skills which most scientists need to learn, and there are enormous benefits. Most people who write and present for public audiences or children subsequently give much better presentations to their scientific colleagues.

FURTHER READING

Nelkin, D. (1995). *Selling Science: How the Press Covers Science and Technology*. New York: W.H. Freeman & Company.

Hutchinson, J. (1998). *Writing for the Press*. London: Hutchinson Educational.

Evered, D. and O'Connor, M. (eds) (1987). *Communicating Science to the Public*. Chichester: Wiley.

Rothwell, N.J. (2000). Show them how it's *really* done. *Nature* **405**: 621.

UK House of Lords (2000). Report on science and society. http://www.publications.parliament.uk, and *Nature* **404**: 211.

Burke, D. (2000). Time for voices to be raised. *Nature* **405**: 509.

12

Power, pressure and politics

When I think of older scientists the picture that forms in my mind is of a committee of grey heads, all confident on the rightness of their opinions and all making pronouncements about the future development of scientific ideas of a kind known by philosophers to be intrinsically unusual.

Most of us enter science because we like doing research. Yet, as we move up in science, achieve success, become respected and recognised, we spend less and less time actually doing experiments and more time managing and directing. But it does not stop there. In academia and industry, further success is likely to mean that you are promoted to positions of influence, which may take you even further away from your lab. The most obvious of these is the position of head of department, which may be rotating and therefore held for just two or three years, or in some cases until retirement, and varies of course depending on the size of the department. Within academia, posts with even wider responsibility include those of dean, institute head, pro-vice chancellor and vice chancellor, and, in industry, equivalent positions may be research director or vice president of research. Those who are chosen for such positions are usually selected on the basis of their success in research rather than their skills at management, but have also proven themselves to be clever, ambitious, organised and hopefully fair. The offer of such a position is very tempting. It brings prestige and respect, responsibility, influence and power, and often a better salary.

WHY BOTHER?

In spite of the apparent attractions of such senior positions, they are not for everyone. Many scientists shy in horror at the thought of being head of department – bringing visions of an endless stream of complaining staff, meetings and paper work, and an end to their beloved research. Other duties, such as editing a journal, chairing a grants panel, heading an academic society or sitting on government bodies, carry similarly heavy work loads that inevitably eat into research time.

Those who choose to take up such positions do so for a variety of reasons. The most altruistic see it as a duty to the scientific community, an exciting challenge bringing new information and understanding and requiring new skills, and hope that they can really have some influence for the good of science. Those who desire such positions simply for the power that they wield are probably least suited as leaders and hopefully will be selected rarely and not reinstated at the end of their terms of office. Some scientists take up senior positions late in their career, when they are becoming rather less research active, and others use them as something of an 'excuse' when their research is running out of steam.

Taking on senior positions whether they are within your own institution or company, national or international, does not necessarily mean giving up your research. But they do mean handling things rather differently. You will need to have an efficient and well-structured lab, usually with one or more senior research staff, ideally in long-term positions, who can direct the day-to-day research. Senior technical staff are needed for managing equipment, stocks, ordering, etc. and a good secretary or administrative assistant is essential (see below). Major responsibilities mean that you will be absent from your research group, sometimes for long periods of time, so the research staff must be able to make decisions for themselves or be able to contact you easily. When time is limited, it is necessary to focus on the important things, which are often the most fundamental – the research direction, the results and the publications. If these are going well, sustaining funding, attracting new staff, successful training of young scientists and maintaining the recognition and reputation of your lab will hopefully follow.

Most senior jobs are undertaken for a period of two to four years. That is usually long enough. It allows you to gain an enormous amount of experience, enjoy the new challenges and have some influence. Unless the job is highly variable and very challenging, or you really find yourself more suited to such a position than to research (in which case a permanent career change may be advisable), three to four years is usually long enough to serve in any senior position. Then it may be time to move on to a new challenge and let someone else with fresh ideas take over. The first year or two is always the hardest, as you are learning what to do. In fact the first three to six months is often a total blur as you seem to be trying desperately hard to just keep up with what is going on. The middle period gets much easier and is the most enjoyable. This is when you are most likely to bring in new innovations and ideas, and actually feel that you are on top of things.

When you are invited to take up a major job, whether this means a change in your career path or something additional, stop and wait for the initial pride to wear off. It is enormously flattering to be invited to act as editor of a journal or chair a grants panel or board. Stop and think, what can you bring to that job and how you can learn and benefit from it. If there are not obvious, positive answers, and if it means you have to give up something that you really enjoy (and do not fool yourself that you can just squeeze it in), politely decline.

LEADERSHIP QUALITIES

It is often claimed that a leader in any company or institution cannot be both really effective and also liked by their staff. I do not agree, since I have met many outstanding heads of department, deans, company research directors and principals who are remarkably effective, but are also liked and admired by their staff. They seem to achieve this by being fair, consulting others wherever possible and by explaining, but not apologising, for their actions. Many of their staff do not like their actions at the time, but recognise (sometimes considerably later) that they were necessary or essential. They usually have little time for formality or favours, treat everyone similarly and always try to spend time *talking* to people and *listening*. They recognise the value of everyone who puts in effort and does a good job, whether they be their deputy or the cleaner, and try to get all staff working together with a sense of collective responsibility and pride in their organisation or department. These are useful lessons, and it is always worth studying your ideal 'role model'.

DELEGATING

The busier you become the more you need to delegate. This is not easy, particularly if you feel (often unjustifiably) that you can do the job better or more quickly than others, that you are giving up things you actually like doing, or that you will lose touch. Successful delegation is a skill which some have or learn better than others. When you have always had to do everything yourself, the idea of getting a secretary or a lab manager is just wonderful. But learning to work with them, ensuring that they can be at their most efficient and know exactly what you are doing and need is not so easy (my secretary still has to battle to extract my diary from me). You may feel awkward asking others to do your work for you, particularly those things that might seem more menial. The best approach is to learn to work together so everyone knows what is needed.

HEAD OF DEPARTMENT

Chairing a department can involve a vast range of duties including appointments, promotions, appraisals, organising and distributing funds, prioritising research, overseeing training for graduate students, representing the department in numerous ways within the institute and outside and dealing with a range of difficult issues from staff complaints and illnesses, to discrimination and dissatisfaction. In industry or research institutes, the head of department will play a major role in directing research, whereas in academia they are likely to have responsibility for teaching, timetables, admission of undergraduates and all aspects of assessment and examination. A fundamental difference between leadership in academia and industry is that in the former faculty staff work largely independently. The head of department can insist that they take on teaching and administrative duties, can determine how much space they have and influence the training of graduate students, but have little or no ability to determine what they work on, who they work with or how they do it. Academic researchers are essentially individuals. This is one of the great attractions of academia for many scientists, but it also has drawbacks. Research in the twenty-first century increasingly requires team work, interaction between staff with complementary skills from different disciplines and sharing of facilities. In industry the head of department (or their bosses) can determine exactly the subject, nature and direction of research.

More senior positions, such as those of dean, vice-chancellor or principal or research director require real breadth of vision and a strategic overview of many aspects of science. These staff will need to see new opportunities for research and training, be in tune with government policies, with the needs of the commercial and academic sector and have the ability to consider multiple disciplines and how they interact.

EDITING JOURNALS

If you have reasonable experience of publishing and reviewing scientific papers, you are likely to be asked at some time to serve on an editorial board. This does not usually entail much work, but expect to receive a significant number of papers to review from that journal. Editorship brings a considerably greater responsibility, which for major journals is a full-time professional job. You will have the responsibility of assessing the reviewers' comments and making the decision of acceptance or rejection of submitted manuscripts, and inevitably will have to handle some very unhappy authors who feel they have been treated unfairly. Editors also have to consider the length and balance of each issue of their journal, the acceptance rate, speed of reviewing and citations (everyone is aiming for high citation rates), and will have to negotiate with the publishers. For some journals, the editor, in consultation with the editorial board, will need to consider invitations for reviews, changes in format and style, and for most journals, now electronic publication. They may also be required to write editorials and to liaise with editors of other journals. One of the hardest aspects of such positions is having to deal with potential cases of plagiarism, justification and fraud or presentation of experiments which might be considered unethical (see Chapter 4).

FUNDING BODIES

Serving on a grant review panel for a major funding body will normally mean reviewing in detail a handful (perhaps half a dozen) of grants in your area, commenting on other proposals at the meeting and probably participating in discussions about other grants and about strategy. The chairman of a grants panel will have to oversee all of these decisions, which means being at least reasonably familiar with each proposal. They will have to ensure each application gets a good hearing, necessary discussion and fair decision and everything is kept on time. For most funding bodies, they will need to do a great deal more besides. Duties may include discussions with staff at the funding body over selection of referees and appropriate board members, contribution to decisions about eligibility of specific applications, feedback to applicants and agreement on costings. For major funding bodies, the chairman may have to deal with anything from studentship or fellowship applications through to programme grants, major proposals and centres, site visits, interviews of staff and involvement in decisions about strategy. The latter is perhaps the most exciting since as a panel or board chairman you can participate in major decisions about new initiatives and directions in research.

All of these activities can take enormous amounts of time and the paperwork may fill half your office. You will almost certainly get support, particularly from the grants officers and support staff at the funding body, and you will need to get to know them well first, trust them and learn to work together as a team.

ACADEMIC STUDIES

For every subject in science there seems to be at least one national and one international society, which varies in size, structure, activity and influence. Some may be small, national groups with a few hundred members and limited resources, usually running just one meeting a year and sending out short newsletters. At the other extreme, those, such as the Society for Neuroscience, have tens of thousands of members, employ a large number of staff and have attendances at the annual meeting of 25,000 or more. Assuming a position on the committee or council of such societies is important and interesting, but again time consuming. Just serving on a committee may not take up too much time. But if you take on positions such as treasurer or meetings secretary, expect a significant commitment. The chairman or president will be responsible not only for overseeing the ongoing activities of the society, but also for looking into the future, moving the society forward, ensuring that it is well positioned for the future, serves the needs of its membership and attracts new members, and is financially stable.

GOVERNMENT COMMITTEES AND LEGISLATIVE BODIES

Most governments have high-level scientific advisors in many aspects of general policy, and also set up specific committees to deal with current issues which might include for example science funding, human cloning, agricultural policy, education in science, etc. Scientists are usually selected on the basis of their standing and expertise in the relevant field, but also for their ability to take a careful and balanced view of complex issues and to deliver considered and impartial answers. Some committees are established to deal with specific needs and can be very much in the public eye.

Scientific advice and expertise is also essential on legislative bodies which regulate or advise on the safety of new medicines, genetic manipulation, cloning, use of human tissue or animals in research and development, food safety, etc. These tend to be sensitive issues, which are likely to attract interest and criticism from the public, the press and the media – mistakes are usually well published. Nevertheless they are important and interesting positions. If you do serve on such committees, you may have to explain or justify the collective decisions of the committee, sometimes to the press or media.

It is easy to duck out of major responsibility, yet stand back and criticise 'the system' – whether it is your own institution, funding body or government policy. If you really want to influence and change things it is probably advisable to get involved, but be aware of the commitment you are facing.

13

Social aspects of science

Hard luck on spouses?

To many people scientists are rather odd. Most of the population look forward to Friday evening – the end of the week – and dread Monday mornings, living in anticipation of the next holiday. Scientists tend to be rather different. They generally like going to work and consider themselves lucky to have a job which is so enjoyable. This is just as well, since success in science is rarely achieved by working from 9 a.m. to 5 p.m., for five days a week. There will be many times when it is necessary to work late into the evenings and at weekends, and to travel to meetings away from home. This of course brings problems for scientists and their families.

PARTNERS AND FAMILIES

The Nobel Prize winner Dorothy Hodgkin commented that one of the most important things for a scientist is to find is a sympathetic and understanding partner; someone who will put up with the many hours you will have to spend in the lab, working on a paper or popping into work at the weekends, which inevitably takes longer than planned; someone who is happy to plan the family holiday around international conferences, to read page after page of thesis or paper and hear talks being practised. There are many jobs that are demanding on time and effort. The competitive areas of business, finance, running your own company, all need commitment outside normal working hours, but in most cases the benefits for your family are a little more obvious. It is not surprising that many scientists partner other scientists who at least know (or should know) about the pressures of research. This can cause difficulties in finding jobs though. Good positions in research are not easy to find, identifying two positions in the same or similar location is even harder. Mobility is particularly important now for a scientific career, and most young scientists expect to spend several years overseas, usually as a post-doc, before finding a secure position. Spouses and partners, therefore, have to move with them and try to find employment in the same place, or put up with several years of long-distance commuting, expensive phone calls and emotional strain. When both are scientists, the scientific locations become more limited.

Children put a great strain on all parents, whatever their career. For scientists (both male and female) it probably means significantly curtailing time at work and limiting trips away. Most academic institutions and companies now offer reasonable maternity leave (and in some countries also paternity leave), job sharing, part-time employment and other options which can help when bringing up small children. But none of this really gets around the problems of the long working hours that are normal in science, and trying to fit the demands of a research career with school holidays and childhood illness.

WOMEN IN SCIENCE

The proportion of male and female undergraduate and even graduate students is reasonably well balanced in many areas of science, with the exception perhaps of some of the physical sciences and engineering. Further up the career ladder there is a marked decline in the proportion of women throughout the world, in academia and commercial science. In the USA only about 10% of full professors are women, in Europe the figure is less than 5%, and in Japan lower still. Female deans, vice-chancellors and directors of research are extremely rare. The number of women in senior positions in science is increasing, but very slowly.

The reasons for this disparity have been analysed extensively, but are complex. Some might argue that women are just less well suited or less able to hold down senior positions in science. This is possible, but not well supported by the evidence. Those women who do succeed appear to do just as well as their male counterparts – sometimes while bringing up a family. The most obvious difficulty is to balance a career in research with family commitments – and indeed many top female scientists do not have children. It would be interesting to analyse whether their choice not to have a family came before or after their decision to go into science, and whether that decision was influenced by career choice. It is difficult to

take a prolonged career break for family reasons and maintain a successful research programme and achieve international recognition. Many
funding bodies now offer fellowships specifically to encourage women
back to research after having a family, and allowance is almost always
made for 'time out' of research when considering CVs. Women should not
feel embarrassed or reticent about mentioning maternity leave or
absences for personal reasons in a CV, and indeed the same should apply
to men. Yet, while the conditions and culture for women with families is
improving slowly, it is still difficult for those with children to maintain
the output of other scientists, to attend meetings which are so often
scheduled before 8.30 a.m. or after 5.30 p.m. or to participate in national
and international meetings. Part-time work helps to meet these conflicting demands but does not solve the problem of what really matters to
your career – your research output.

There are probably a number of other reasons for the low numbers
of women in senior positions in science, which may also apply to the even-
more serious under-representation of certain ethnic minorities. Mentors
and role models are very important, and there are still relatively few
senior women, or scientists from non-caucasian backgrounds, to act as
such role models. Women questioned about the problems they face in
science suggest that men are naturally more confident, assertive and out-
going and that these factors contribute to their success in science, while
women are less likely to promote themselves. It is difficult to determine
whether these comments are reflected in reality, and indeed whether
confidence and assertiveness have a significant effect on success in
science. It could be argued that women have other attributes which help
them succeed.

Discrimination, on the basis of gender, age, ethnicity, culture or
religion occurs in all walks of life. We like to think that it is rare in the scientific world, but we cannot ignore the fact that scientists, as humans,
are likely to exhibit some discriminatory behaviour, however unintentional. Great efforts are now made by all institutions, companies and
funding bodies and other groups in science to limit discrimination. If you
believe you have had experience of discrimination, whether directly or
directed towards others, it should be discussed with a senior colleague.

Success in science is largely dependent on productivity. You may be
viewed as an excellent scientist but it is what is on paper (your CV) which
really matters. Your publications, peer reviewed funding, invitations to
international meetings and other esteem indicators are what matters
when it comes to jobs, position, grants, etc. Therefore those making the

assessments will not always take account (or even know) of family com-mitments, so it is worth mentioning these in your CV. Though there are attempts to change this.

Some countries now operate 'positive discrimination' in an attempt to selectively promote the appointment of minority groups. But this has disadvantages as well as advantages. Many members of these minority groups are not in favour of positive discrimination, and the practice can 'dilute' quality. It can also, inadvertently, lead to high work loads for those that are being promoted. Those organising meetings, setting up committees or allocating major jobs want to ensure that they have at least some women and if possible (though very hard to find) some members from a non-caucasian background. This means that the minor-ity groups may get a better chance in some aspects of science, but will also have more duties.

SOCIAL RELATIONSHIPS

Research involves working closely with people in teams, collaborating with other scientists from all over the world and meeting up regularly with colleagues at conferences. It is therefore likely that you will make many lifelong friends in science. Such friends may be valuable to you in the future, but be careful what you ask of them and how you deal with friends in the work arena. You cannot expect them (or them of you) to provide a better than honest personal reference, or review of your paper or grant, or treat you any differently to people they have never met – and nor can you deal with friends any differently. If you feel tempted to do so, declare a conflict of interest and back out.

Husband and wife teams are quite common in science. Spouses may work together in the same department or the same lab on the same project. This arrangement usually works well. But a few institutions are reluctant to employ relatives in the same department and occasionally marital relationships can lead to tensions. They can lead to the inevitable concern over conflict of interest (it is very hard for someone to act totally impartially to their spouse or family member) and confidentiality. This is not to say that close relatives should not and cannot work successfully together, but they and their colleagues need to be aware of potential conflicts.

FURTHER READING

Lawler, A. (1999). Tenured women battle to make it less lonely at the top. *Science* **286**: 1272–8.

Wanneras, C. and Wold, A. (1997). Nepotism and sexism in peer review. *Nature* **387**: 341–3.

Rothwell, N.J. (1999). Why so few? Nobel Prize women in science: their struggles and momentous achievements. *Bioessays* **21**: 892–3.

14

So who does want to be a scientist?

Among scientists are collectors, classifiers and compulsive tidy uppers, many are detectives by temperament and many are explorers; some are artists and others are artisans. There are poet scientists and philosopher scientists and even a few mystics.

Maybe it is hard to decide if you want to be a scientist because there are so many aspects to science, and scientists do so many different things. As Medawar noted (above) scientists come in every shape and form. The stereotypical scientist – the 'man' of logic, careful judgement and assessment who has a logical view of the world, sets up hypotheses and then tests them – is far from reality. Successful science demands imagination, and insight, sensitivity and common sense, as well as a passion for discovery.

This book has, by necessity, focussed on the potential problems faced by scientists moving up their careers, and has tried to provide some advice. Most scientists will hopefully encounter few, if any, of these problems and will rely simply on their own drive and initiative, on friends and colleagues and a sense of fair play. To highlight the potential problems may lead to a rather pessimistic view of research, which is not well founded. Few scientists encounter serious cases of fraud or plagiarism, unfairness or unwillingness to share, discrimination or prejudice. For the most part, the scientific community is remarkably open, friendly and welcoming – and a pleasure to work with. Some of the issues mentioned in this book are ones which you should be prepared for, but do not look for them around every corner.

A training in science provides one of the best groundings for almost any career – providing not only practical and intellectual skills, but also training in ways to think and act. Not everyone who believes they want to enter a career in science will follow this path, but hopefully they will benefit from the experience. Those who do stay in science may end up doing many different things. Only a few will become rich, less will become famous, but most, hopefully, will enjoy their work and consider themselves fortunate to have such enjoyable employment.

Many successful students do not realise what they want to do until quite late. The usual school education, an undergraduate degree and even some postgraduate training in science does not necessarily provide the real highs and lows of research. But if you really get the bug you will know, and may decide that you really do want to be a scientist.

FURTHER READING

Medawar, P. (1961). *The Strange Case of the Spotted Mice*. Oxford: Oxford University Press.

Index

academic career 76
academic positions 77
accuracy
  measurement 18
achievements
  career 81
acknowledgements
  in publications 46, 52
  in talks 65
administration duties 100
administrative assistance 12
animal experimentation 36, 42
  grants 114
  public appreciation 142
applied research 123
appraisal 98
assessment
  promotion 98
attitude to research 9
audience
  grant application 109–10
audio-visual presentation 63
author position
  on papers 50
authorship 52
awards 82

basic research 123
Batchelor's degree 6
bias
  experimental 31
biomedical research 78
blind analysis
  data 32
'borons' 65
British Association (UK) 140
bureaucracy
  institutional 101

career
  alternative 79–80

career break 82
career progression 40, 71–2, 98, 101
Chair
  departmental 77
children
  effect on research 155
citation
  of research papers 30
CNRS (France) 78
collaboration
  academia–industry 130
Collaboration
  research 71, 74, 83, 101
commercial development
  research results 133
committee
  scientific 147
communication 39, 57
competition
  with boss 90
conduct 29
confidentiality 131
  patent 128
conflict of interest 30, 158
consultancy 132
contingency planning
  grant application 107
contract
  short-term 73
contract research 131
control
  experimental 14, 15
copyright permission 33
critique
  scientific 48
curriculum vitae 80–3

data
  analysis 23, 96
  manipulation 24, 32
  presentation 23, 25

data (*cont.*)
  recording 22
  variation 23
deadlines
  article 21
  grant application 109
deduction
  scientific 25
delegation 149
department head (Chief) 150
diary
  experiments 18
  time-management 21
directing research 89–91
disclosure (public domain) 125, 128
discrimination 36, 157

editor
  journal 53, 150
enemies 83
ethics 29
examiner
  thesis 48
examination
  Ph.D. 97
experiment
  optimisation of 15
experimental data 23
experimental design 13–14, 25, 96
  grant application 112
experimental technique 16

family 155
fellowships 75
filing system 19, 23
financial management 100
Fleming, Alexander 17
fraud 34–6
funding 46, 72, 90, 105, 151
  start-up 77

government committee 152
grant application 14, 41, 90, 106–19
grant review panel 151

habilitation (Germany) 77
harrassment 36
Health and Safety regulations 12
holidays 12
hosting
  seminar speaker 68
Howard Hughes Medical Institute 78
Human Frontiers Science Programme
  (International) 108
hypothesis 13–14, 27, 31
  grant application 108

impact factor 51, 81
independence 72, 89–90

research 82
indirect costs
  grant 118
industry
  funding sources 116
  research options in 78
information sharing 124
INSERM (France) 78
intellectual property
  ownership of 131
intellectual property rights 125
interpersonal skills 92, 99
interview
  job 83–6
interview panel 84
interview technique 84
interviewing staff 93–5
invention 127

job fair 66
job security 74
journal
  editing 150
  scientific 50

Karolinska Institutet (Sweden)
  78

laboratory
  life 11
  management 100
  notebook 18, 23, 128
  rules 95
  support 20
laboratory head (Chief) 11, 34
  management of 21
leadership 34, 91, 149
learned societies 152
lecture 58
lecturer 77
literature
  scientific 45
luck
  experimental 17

management
  financial 100
  laboratory 100
  people 91
Master's degree 6
Material Transfer Agreement
  patents 132
Max Planck Institute 78
measurements
  experimental 16
Medical Research Council (UK) 78
mentor 2, 5, 43
mentoring 73
misconduct 29, 31, 34

National Institutes of Health (USA) 108
National Science Foundation (USA) 108
networking 57, 83
networking
    at a meeting 67
null hypothesis 13

objectivity
    experimental 32
observation
    experimental 13–14
Office of Scientific Integrity (USA) 34,
    36
online publications 45
organisation
    seminar 67
ownership
    ideas 129

paperwork
    as records 19
part-time work 157
partner
    understanding 155
patent application 129
patents 125, 126
peer review 50, 55
Personal Assistant
    of senior scientist 22
personality 9
personality clash 20
Ph.D. project 6
plagiarism 32
politics 147–53
post-doctoral research 72
post-doctoral staff 12
poster presentation 59
power analysis 24
PowerPoint® presentation 64
pragmatism
    in experiments 15
preliminary experiment 24
presentation
    audio-visual 57, 63
    grant application 114
    oral 57
    poster 33, 44
    PowerPoint® 64
    radio 44
    scientific 33, 34
    television 144
press release 143
prioritisation 19
priority
    patent/invention 127
prizes 82
productivity
    research 157
programme grant 116

project grant 116
Promotion 98
public awareness of science
    137–45
public domain (disclosure) 125
public speaking 139
publication record 9, 81
Publishing
    scientific papers 39

radio presentation 144
Reader 77
reading 46
referees
    journal 45, 53, 54
    personal in CV 82
referees
    job 93
    journal 53, 54
reference
    bibliographical 44
rejection
    grant application 116
reprimand 99
Research Councils (UK) 108
research
    excellence 8
    institutions 78
    project 11
    teamwork 30
Research Assessment Exercise 7
review panel
    grant 151
reviewer
    grant application 115–18
reviews (scientific) 46
rules
    laboratory 12, 95
rules of conduct 29

salary expectations
    industry 78
school children
    presentation to 140–1
science as a career vii, 2
scientific administration 41
scientific critique 26
scientific discussion 25
Scientific Integrity
    Office of 34, 36
scientific literature 45
scientific meeting 66
scientific philosophy 13
scientist
    stereotypical 161
secretarial assistance 12
secretary of senior scientists 22
self-citation 30
seminar 18, 58

skills
  presentational 1
slides
  visual presentation 61
sloppiness
  and presentation of data 44
socialising 21
spouse
  understanding of 155, 158
stakeholder
  academic research 121
start-up companies 78
statistical analysis 23
statistical significance
  of results 24
supervision 92
  graduate students 95
supervisor 2, 5, 8, 21, 43,
  choice of 7
  conflicts with 22
  constructive criticism from 45

teaching 41, 76, 83
teamwork
  research 30
technical assistance
  laboratory 12

scientific articles 52
technique
  experimental 16, 17
technology transfer 125
television presentation 144
tenure 76
thesis 40–1, 47
thinking 13, 17–19, 96
time-management 19
training course 96
travel costs
  grants 114
tutor 8

undergraduate students
  work experience 12

variation
  experimental 18, 31
viva voce
  Ph.D. examination 49, 97

Wellcome Trust (UK) 108
women in science 156–8
word processing 44
working hours 12, 18, 155
writing 39, 43, 48